The Animal Lovers' Bedtime Reader

by
Sue Greenall

ACKNOWLEDGMENTS

Horses and the many accompanying creatures have carried me through the toughest times in life and surely without them I would have faltered. I have laughed and cried with them, shared their secrets and been privileged to be part of their inner world. Giving them life again in the pages of this book has acknowledged how much they have given me. And then there is the husband who supported, encouraged and rallied me whenever needed.

Edited by Marsha Himler
Technical assistance by Dinah Rojek, Jo Steele
and Mary Ann Barcellona
Cover painting by Beth Carlson
(Aleser, Willie Wonka, Girlfrien', Nudge & Strubbles)
Illustrated by the pets

The Animal Lovers' Bedtime Reader
Copyright 2008 by Susan Greenall
All Rights Reserved

Printed in the United State of America
Printed by R.C. Brayshaw & Company, Inc
ISBN# 978-1-4276-3689-8

Please consider adopting your next pet

For additional copies
Greenall@vermontel.net
www.vermontel.com/~greenall

The Animal Lovers' Bedtime Reader

Kitties on the Keyboard

When I first sat down to write, so many years ago, I was just a kid. I had been sufficiently inspired by my adventures with animals but the trick for me was getting the stories onto paper. My chronically bad penmanship and my unique grammar style presented a problem (still does). I signed up for High School Typing 1, hoping it would at least improve the readability of my work, but found myself to be an equally sloppy typist. Aside from the elimination of the nasty little clicks that manual machines make (a real point of contention between me and a ferret that lived in the second drawer down on the right in my desk years later), the introduction of electric typewriters only made my backspacing and retyping faster.

I did manage to get some stories written, pecking on the keyboard into the night with a dictionary balanced on my knees and faithful interruption from the cats. Click, click, stroke, click, stroke, backspace, click, boom! Down would fall the dictionary and zoom would go the cats.

The invention of word processors and built-in spell checks was like throwing a life raft to a drowning person. At last I could backspace and type over my mistakes without having to suffer the consequences of White Out. Finally, I could move my legs without a six-pound dictionary crashing to the floor. I couldn't wait to plug the thing in.

However, I still had a problem with the cats. To a cat, your time is their time. The nice warm surface of a computer offered up an inviting place to nap. My typing was bad enough without the windshield wiper of a cat's tail jerking across my monitor screen. The desk drawers offered a place for a nice little cat nap (except for the second drawer down on the right where the ferret lived). My notes were a great place to plop down for a visit. And the keyboard was still an ideal place for stroking a cat between sentences. Type, type, stroke, type, backspace, type, stroke, type.

My best writing was on rainy days, with the ratta-tap-tap on the roof, a fire warming my back and a cat on my lap. Periodically, they would pop out the cat door to check on the weather for me, racing back in with their wet little paws to show me that it was, indeed, still raining. Cats expect a little attention for performing such services. Cats, fortunately, have little working knowledge of computers (although Kitty Carlisle did manage to rename one of my documents). Walking across the keyboard of a computer presents an entirely different scenario than walking on a typewriter. Then there is the issue of cat hair. Inspection of the inside of my computer showed that I had more than the recommended amount rolling around in there. Twenty cats later, I am finally done; however the presence of kitties at my keyboard has slowed my work by at least ten years.

One Dark and Rainy Night...

Long before the farm in Vermont with beautiful horses running in the pastures along with a goat and a goose guarded by faithful dogs who happily shared with barn cats and house cats who played with a ferret and a fish, I was a kid with dreams of such. From the moment my mother placed me in my playpen I wanted the cat in there too. I cried for days when the duck became dinner in "Journey to the Center of the Earth". With my face pressed against the window of our car I would hope for just a fleeting glimpse of a horse in a field. Given the opportunity to stand near, touch or smell a horse, I was filled with joy, then longed for yet another encounter. I was an addict from birth and was destined to live a life filled with cat hair and horse manure. I can remember nothing else.

It was the middle of the night, or so it seemed, when the phone rang. It was the police. I didn't know it was the police until my father gruffly woke me and said it was for me.

"It's the police," he grunted. "Something about your horses", delivered in a tone that said – why aren't you like other girls who date boys instead of spending all of your time in a barn with animals that get out in the middle of the night and cause the police to wake up people who don't even like horses so that they can get you out of bed for some wild goose chase while I lie awake for the rest of the night wondering where you are?

He seemed to have forgotten that he bought me the horse so I wouldn't date boys in the first place and have to lie awake all night wondering where I was. How was he to know that one horse would turn into three, if you count the pony as a whole number, and that I would go through high school and college without a significant relationship with the opposite sex. Even at this point in time, he, and I, did not know that I would not get married until I was thirty-five. But at this point I was scarcely twenty-one and living back home for that awkward period between college and a real job. In truth, I was having a grand time playing with the horses.

3

The phone call informed me that a squad car would be picking me up in a matter of minutes so that I could collect my equines who were stomping hoof prints all over Mrs. Gorka's nice green lawn. It was summer and I was clad in but a set of pink baby doll pajamas, which I managed to cover with a shirt of my fathers as I dashed out the door.

The squad car pulled to a halt at the house and the door opened rather unceremoniously for me to get in. Which I did. Perhaps it was the hour or perhaps it was being ripped from a peaceful sleep that I thought I recognized the cop sitting next to me as the same person I sat next to in high school Algebra I. No way! The kid next to me in Algebra I was a real geek. Glasses, high water pants and a nasty case of acne. He used to cheat off my test papers all the time even though I tried my best to keep him from doing so. But I would get engrossed in a problem and suddenly I would feel his eyes all over my paper. I would look up, but he always managed to appear busy with his pencil. I doubt I ever said two words to him the entire semester. I never saw him again. He must have moved away or something. But I did remember his name.

As we sped down the road towards the saving of Mrs. Gorkas lawn, he introduced himself. Oh my ears and whiskers…it was him! Perhaps the darkness of the night was hiding the glasses, the high water pants and the acne. But I didn't think so. Sitting beside me was a tall, very fit and very good looking young man? Oh, boy. Perhaps when he moved away he had a hormone implant.

Now I wondered if he recognized me. Well, of course he did, he knew my name before he came to pick me up. Oh my. Now I was wishing that I had let him cheat. So, the only thing to do was jump right in with, " so what have you been doing between Algebra I and a squad car?"

He threw me a dashing grin, oh my, and replied, "my father was in the military so this was a logical step."

Aha, that is what happened to him, military school! To this day I remain impressed with what they did with that boy.

We arrived at Mrs. Gorka's house to find her standing under the porch light in her bathrobe.

"They went that way," she shrieked. "I heard them about half an hour ago thundering through here like a herd of buffalo. They circled the house three times then took off towards Mr. Kusmas. He has roses you know."

I shuddered at her accurate description of the antics my horses were known to perform. The leader was my cute little pony who was black as night and had the lips of Houdini. He could escape almost anything but, not liking to go it alone, would take it upon himself to release the latches of the other horse enclosures so as to ensure company during a nightly raid of the neighborhood. Mrs. Gorka and I were no strangers.

I assured Mrs. Gorka that I would be back in the morning to stomp in the divots caused by my marauding equine's hooves. Even in the dim light of the porch, I could see that it would be a day's project. As we hopped back into the squad car toward the last seen direction of the trio, it started to rain. Great. I was not thinking so much about getting wet, I was thinking of the addition of skid marks to the divots. I would be out stomping down lawns for days.

Mr. Kusmas house was over the hill. The horses took the direct route; we had to take the road which was the long route around. This allowed for driving time during which my Algebra I classmate-turned-super-cop started a conversation.

"I wasn't sure you would remember me," he started, "but I am glad that you did. I want to apologize for trying to cheat from you in Algebra."

Just what do you say to that? "It's OK, I didn't mind?" or how about "You were trying to cheat, I never noticed!" Instead I said, rather stupidly, "it happens all the time." Duh. He didn't notice and went on to tell me where he had been and how he got to be a cop. Every so often I would manage a peek at him and simply marvel at the change.

When we arrived at Mr. Kusma's, the place was dark. I rolled down the window in order to hear any telltale horsy noises. Nothing. I had grabbed several ropes and halters while dashing out the door, but nothing else. No can of grain to shake to grab their attention away from Mr. Kusma's roses. No apples or carrots or peppermints in my fathers' shirt pocket. Why would a man who didn't like horses have apples or carrots or peppermints in his shirt pocket?

So I turned to super-cop and asked, "would you happen to have a can of grain or any carrots or apples or peppermints?"

He looked back at me, stunned by the request. To be sure, he had never been asked that before. Life saving equipment, yes. Crowd control apparatus, yes. He even had a body board. But I wanted a can. Or an apple. Or a carrot. However, by some stroke of luck, he happened to have some peppermints on the console of the squad car. I was in business.

Do you know anything about horses?" I asked as we started into the darkness with me fingering the cellophane on a peppermint.

"Actually I do," he replied, "my sister had horses". He had a sister? Boy, did I not pay attention in high school.

"The pony will hear the wrinkling of the cellophane on the peppermint, " I explained, " and he will do anything for a peppermint."

He nodded, as if he knew that.

Ten seconds later I bumped smack into a horse butt. With the rain and it being dark, it wasn't at all hard to do. It was a rather large horse butt and it was connected to a rather large horse. I didn't own any large horses. My pony was small, really small. He was of the perfect height so that if you bumped into him in the dark, as I had this one, one would catapult head over heals over his back and land on your face. Been there, done that. My two horses were not only small, they were white. You would have to be totally blind to bump into them even on a dark and rainy night.

These were not my horses! When I shared this fact with my new friend the super-cop, we both had a good laugh.

"Well, just whose horses are these then," he queried?

Good question. Just because I was the proud owner of three horses, if you counted the pony as a whole number, it did not mean that I knew every horse in town. Just then it started to really rain and I was thinking of how nice it would be to get home to my nice warm bed and finish out the night undisturbed AND not have to get up the next morning to stomp down all of the divots on Mrs. Gorka's lawn.

All hopes of that dashed when he said, with all the charm of a super-cop, "give me a helping hand here." Then smiled at me with a "I would like to get to know you better" look.

Not fair, not fair at all! I was left with no choice but to comply. With the halters and leads I had brought we collected up the horses who were happily munching in Mr. Kusma's roses. Boy, was I exultant they were not my horses. I was making a mental note to give my guys extra treats in the morning simply for not being here tonight.

Several radio calls to the police station brought two more squad cars, which in a town our size made up the entire police force. Luck would have it that a friends' husband was on that night and took special delight in finding me standing in wet pink baby doll pajamas holding three big horses. I refused to respond to his comments.

Several more radio calls discovered the owner of the trampling trio, a new person to the area who had been out looking for her darlings since dark. I couldn't wait to introduce her to Mrs. Gorka! It was decided that the fastest route of return was back over the hill. "Just ride them back," chirped the owner, "the two mares are pussycats."

Easy for her to say, she was not wearing wet pink baby doll pajamas with no underwear. My getting-wetter-by-the-minute fathers' shirt was barely doing the job. Up to this point I had been pretty good at avoiding the squad car headlights, but my situation with the clinging baby dolls was getting serious. It became very clear to me that riding a horse bareback in the dark was looking better than climbing into a squad car with "one of the boys" and having to live that one down for the rest of my life.

So I agreed to do it.

Pussycat #1 stood quiet as could be when I was launched up onto her back. I could not see what Pussycat #2 did when super-cop vaulted onto her back because she took off like a rocket. Supercop and all. I had hold of horse #3 who stood quietly, uninterested, along with Pussycat #1, over the disappearance of their mate. We just stood there, three cops, two horses and me; staring dumbfounded into the darkness, wondering what to do next. Suddenly, super-cop reappeared, somewhat shaken, uniform now with a big mud stain, but with #2 firmly gripped in hand.

Seems that super-cop hadn't checked the sex of his "Pussycat" when he leapt onto it's back …#2 was an unridden baby two year old gelding…oops. We made the correction and the trip over the hill had no further incidents. I got to bed, after a long hot shower to remove umpteen horse hairs from my inner thighs, at a decent hour but not before giving #1, #2, and #3 a peppermint each for getting me off the hook with Mrs. Gorka.

Oh, and I dated the super-cop several times before realizing that you can't take the geek out of a man, military school or not.

The Extras

The primary impulse people have, after moving to their first farm, is to fill it with livestock. What starts out as impulse, ends up as an odd ball group of animals, many of whom the "newbie" owner hasn't a clue as to their purpose. They are "the extras".

In my case, the first to arrive were the ducks at Easter, when else? They had started out in a basket lined with purple plastic grass to the delight of a four-year-old child and the horror of her mother. "Of course I will take them", I declared when asked to give them a home. They were in my kitchen by sundown.

The two little yellow fuzzballs lived in my bathtub for a month. They turned out to be Muscovy ducks. Muscovies are the ugliest, clumsiest nastiest ducks on webbed feet. They get large red wattles on their faces, move like an ocean liner out of water, their heads jerking to and fro like a mechanical toy weighing thirty pounds. Usually people eat them out of self-defense before that happens. The silliest thing about them is that no matter how big or how old they get, they still peep! Imagine a thirty-pound duck saying, "peep!"

Twiddle Dee Dee and Twiddle Dee Dum were the names that fittingly stuck to my well-fed thirty-pound ducks. By the following Spring they showed a lot of interest in making more ducks which left Dee on her eggs and Dum with nothing much to do.

Yet another phone call had produced another "extra", a pygmy goat named Benny Hill. My livestock acquisitions were growing along with my reputation for being a sucker who would take any hoofed or winged creature off someone's hands. Benny was a rather shy goat, his main motive to stay out of, rather than get into, trouble.

The ducks and Benny Hill shared the stacked bales of hay as a place to nap and hang out. But when Dee settled down for nesting, Dum decided that the area was simply not big enough for the three of them so he chased poor Benny out. I would think that a healthy goat with horns wouldn't be afraid of a dumb duck, but this duck, Dum the Muscovy, was so ugly that Benny ran for his life.

Dum liked the idea of running. He followed Benny in hot pursuit.

Running ducks are pretty entertaining to watch. Around the barn, under the fence, through my garden, across the porch, back to the barn they went. Finally, leaping atop the hay bales, Benny was safe. He had little choice but to stay up there as Dum paced back and forth at the bottom just daring Benny to try to run for it again. This was Dum's kind of game!

Ducks sit on their eggs for twenty-eight days. For twenty-eight days Dum had nothing other to do than keep Benny atop the hay bales. Whenever Benny came down, there was the mad dash for the door followed by the chase around the farm. Should poor Benny slow his pace enough for Dum to catch the hairs on Benny's behind in his beak, we were treated to the sight of a duck in half flight sailing along behind a goat who was trying to run and sit at the same time. Before long, Benny's poor little behind began to look quite plucked.

Twiddle Dee Dum gained confidence. He started to look about for bigger and better game. He found it in my housemate, Peggy. Peggy was a bit nervous about big ugly ducks that peeped and he sensed that. One morning as she left for work, Dum left his post at the bottom of the hay and stuck his head out of the barn door to watch Peggy walk the fifty yards to her truck. Suddenly inspired, he flew from the barn, neck outstretched, wings beating the ground in rhythm with his feet as he propelling himself toward her leg. Naturally, she ran screaming.

Dum thought this a noble game, so the next morning he did it again. That evening Peggy started looking up recipes for duck.

"You're afraid of a dumb duck?", I asked.

No response.

"It's just a game with him, just like with the goat." That didn't get a response either. I was beginning to realize that Peggy shared many of poor Benny's feelings about Dum.

Feeling somewhat responsible for her plight, I offered up a solution. "You simply need to make him respect you," With that, a sinister light came into Peggy's eyes.

For some time Peggy had tried to sneak out the door before Dum saw her, but it always ended up as a mad dash for the safety of her truck. It's amazing she didn't manage to run him over with the truck as she tore out the drive. All the while, a plan was forming in Peggy's mind, one she pondered over and over each night before she fell asleep. She was going to get that dumb duck!

All that week Peggy tried to outsmart Dum, but it always ended up the same. She would arise earlier and earlier and park her truck closer and closer to the house. Creeping about the kitchen as quietly as possible so not to tip off Dum to her presence, she would keep a watchful eye on the barn door. Carefully, ever so carefully, she would slip through the screen door, trying to avoid the tell tale "squeak" that screen doors are so famous for. Sometimes she got the head start, sometimes Dum did, and the race was on. Peggy screaming duck obscenities, Dum peeping them back.

Peggy had had enough. The day of reckoning was to be Saturday, the logic being that Dum would not expect her to be leaving for work. The fact that Peggy gave the duck credit for keeping track of the days of the week worried me. Her plan was to climb out the front window so that Dum wouldn't be tipped off by the squeak of the screen door. Peggy could then sneak up on Dum, grab him from behind, then give him a thorough shaking and lecture about respect.

Plans never work out the way you expect them to. First, Dum didn't know it was Saturday. Second, Peggy was a big girl. It took a long time for her to hoist herself through that window, all the while muttering something about never liking Daffy Duck or Donald Duck or Peking Duck in the first place. Despite her planned efforts, Dum was waiting for her.

As she tentatively strode towards the barn door, he was heading out through the same. They collided in the doorway. Peggy made a gallant attempt at grabbing him. Unfortunately for her, the big toe of her right foot, which was wearing a flip flop (truly the weak link in her plan), caught on an uneven section of the cement floor. The cement ripped into her big toe nail as she landed flat on her behind. Dum totally surprised, sailed right over her. It must have been beautiful to watch.

Regardless of Peggy's feelings, I still liked that duck. Life returned to normal on the farm and Peggy kept in touch after she moved out. No hard feelings on either side, but she did mail me her toenail when it finally fell off. When the ducklings hatched, we kept two, S.O.D. (Son of Dum) and Diddle Diddle Dum who grew up to be ugly Muscovies just like their parents.

The Flying Wallenda

My first farm came with chickens. Clever deal, selling the chickens with the farm, a whole lot easier than trying to catch them. There were six black Bantam hens who had, for generations, lived wild in the barn. I liked chickens, but these girls were turkey vulture ugly.

Naturally, the offer of a fancy rooster from yet another "friend", who was on to my need to acquire livestock, seemed a perfect solution. I named him The Wizard of Oz and he was truly beautiful. His neck had a collar of silky orange feathers that blended into a golden body which was topped off by a flowing ebony tail. The contrast he made against those black hens made them seem even uglier.

He got to work the very first day by rounding up his girls and assigning them places to roost at night and organizing little scratch and peck outings during the day. By the time I had the horses settled into the barn, I thought I had the chicken situation under control.

My first hint of trouble was that the hens refused to lay their eggs in the nice new nesting boxes I had procured for them. They preferred the phone, the saddles, or the horses feed buckets, thank you very much. The horses adapted quite well to this turn of events, being able to eat all of their grain, yet leave a somewhat sticky egg behind. On occasion I would make the mistake of feeding the horses just as a hen was laying her egg. Two pounds of feed landing on top of a humorless black hen caused a feathery eruption out of the bucket accompanied by a tirade of chicken obscenities.

One morning I noticed one of the horses was pacing his stall instead of eating his grain. Concerned I watched closer only to see him walk to the bucket, carefully stick his nose down, then jump back in terror. I couldn't imagine what was wrong until I peered over the edge to see a tiny but determined hen sitting on her egg. Her pint-sized pecks were holding off a nine hundred pound horse from having his breakfast. I had little choice but to add a second bucket.

It took countless generations before the chickens Whiz sired stopped being ugly. Happily, they inherited Whiz's friendly personality and started acting like chickens rather than turkey vultures.

I named one outstanding young rooster The Flying Wallenda. The Wallenda family was perhaps the most daring of all the high wire artists in their feats above the ground, billing themselves as the famous "Flying Wallendas." His name was well earned.

My young rooster was about half grown when his mother left him and his siblings to fend for themselves. There were two hens and The Whiz who squeezed into the tight quarters on the roost, leaving little Wallenda and his pals to find lodging elsewhere. The problem was not easily solved, as the windowsill was too narrow, the sliding door unpredictable and the hay too open.

While his friends reluctantly opted for the hay, our hero spied a spot no one else seemed to have noticed. High above the floor and reaching halfway across the barn ran a loosely hung extension cord that was no longer in use. Wallenda spotted it. It was no easy trick getting up there. The cord hung down eight inches from the ceiling, necessitating a "ducked" landing. Little Wallenda made many attempts to perfect the landing, and he finally did it.

Once landed, he was faced with the problem of how to stay put. With just a swinging wire in his talons, Wallenda had quite a balancing act to perform. As the wire swung forward, Wallenda swung back and, as the wire swung back, Wallenda pitched forward. He looked very much like those plastic birds on a swing that can be put on an infants crib. Once he got that wire under control, he was smugly content. Not only was he as high as the other birds, he didn't have to share his space. No one else wanted to go through that much effort to join him.

Every night, when the chickens went to roost, Wallenda flew up to his high wire. Every night he swung to and fro, to and fro, until the wire settled down. I began to appreciate his agility when one night I stepped into the barn and threw on the lights, causing instant havoc among the sleeping chickens. Poor Wallenda shot straight up sending the wire into wild contortions, but he stayed put.

Once, one of the youngsters sleeping in the hay decided to join Wallenda on his wire. His repeated, and unsuccessful, attempts to fly up caused Wallenda no end of rocking and rolling. Thank goodness the youngster got over that idea quickly.

My father, trying to be helpful, tacked Wallenda's wire securely to the ceiling. We had to take part of it back down again for fear that Wallenda would seriously injure himself trying to land on a wire that was not there.

As with any star performer, Wallenda worked on improving his act. We had grown used to the high wire rooster, so what? But when he brought the horse into the act, he again got our attention. Wallenda started by flying up onto the horse's back. At just the right spot, he would scurry up the neck and perch between the horse's ears. I can't imagine what the horse was thinking. Wallenda would hesitate just long enough for the full effect, then burst off in a flutter of feathers to the high wire. His audience went wild and The Flying Wallenda received the standing ovations he so deserved.

Bandits in the House

I was teaching summer school. No one likes summer school, especially the teacher. Being trapped in a hot and sticky classroom with twenty hot and sticky teenagers, who could have written a thousand word essay on "What I'd Rather be Doing at this Very Minute," was not my idea of how to spend my summer. It was, however, the only way to keep the horses fed and a roof over their heads. The things I did for animals!

It was just another hot and sticky day until Marie paraded into my class followed by two tiny, but very mobile, raccoons. Marie, one of my former students, shared my love of all creatures, large and small. I hope she will someday write a book of her own adventures. The two raccoons offered a welcome excuse to stop class. The twenty failing biology students, Marie and I spent the rest of the morning playing on the floor with our little guests.

I knew better than to ask where Marie had gotten the raccoons. I also knew better than to ask why she had brought them to my classroom. In the ten years that I taught the sciences, my office was endowed with hooded rats, mice, cats, puppies, chickens, pigeons, hamsters, fish, skunks, ferrets, an especially friendly tarantula, and a not so friendly vole by my students. Marie, willing to keep only one raccoon, offered me the wilder one, the female called Raquel. I never could resist turning down deals such as this, so I was soon learning all about raccoons in the car on the way home.

Referring to Raquel as the wilder of the two was a bit of an understatement. Her brother, Rocky, adjusted to his human home like a pig in a cornfield. He shed his raccoon clothing and became a cat or dog or anything you wanted him to be as long as he was fed. Raquel, on the other hand, had drawn a firm line between her "raccooness" and other species. She was willing to take the care and food that she needed to survive, but she knew deep down that she would grow to be a raccoon, nothing else. For that, I could do no more than respect and admire her. So, while Marie spent that first year cuddling and playing with Rocky, I adjusted my life to fit the requirements of a raccoon.

Baby raccoons require little more than food and protection in the beginning, but then their needs multiply. What Raquel needed the most, after separating from Rocky, was companionship, which she found in the form of my kitten, Killer MacKenzie. Killer delighted in the arrival of a masked "kitty" to the household, showing her his litter box and bowl of cat food with pride. While Raquel opted to forgo the litter box, she did develop a passion for cat food from the start. In fact, Purina would be happy to know that I raised a healthy and robust raccoon on their product.

Raquel required a cage when I was not at home, which didn't bother her since she spent the day sleeping. My arrival home from summer school didn't rouse her interest one bit. Since her nocturnal schedule gave me little time to "play" with her, I tried to make her first waking hours worth spending with me by appealing to her basic instincts. I fed her.

We had such interesting discovery time with foods. I was astonished to find Raquel an extremely picky eater. Although interested in food as a play toy, she dismissed each tidbit by rolling it into a squashy little ball before dropping it on my floor. Allowing her to have a bowl of water in order for her to "wash" her food, like all those stories we've heard about, produced wet, squashy balls of food on my floor. I tried lettuce, apples, pears, carrots, tomatoes, fresh fish, frozen fish and live fish, all of which ended up as squashy little balls on my floor. Through my sheer persistence, she settled on three acceptable foods: Purina cat chow (no other brand would do), green California seedless grapes, and bananas, none of which could be found in the natural habitat of a raccoon in Eastern Pennsylvania.

Raquel slept all day, waking just in time for me to say good night to her. This way her raccoon/human time was at a minimum. Killer, also a nocturnal creature by nature, obliged by sleeping most of the day with her (however, periodic cat romps interrupted his nap when the other felines of my household decided to have an impromptu soccer match in my living room.)

We soon developed an acceptable routine. I would offer her my newest variety of raccoon food, which she would roll into squashy little balls before they ended up on the floor. I would then turn on the laundry sink faucet and the three of us would play "splash the wall," a complex,

but highly entertaining game that raccoons, cats and demented humans like to play late into the night. I would then bid them good night, and turn the laundry room over to the antics of two creatures who, by God's great design, were never intended to spend an evening together.

Raquel never, never left the laundry room. As if she had drawn an invisible line between her world and mine, the laundry door way was never to be crossed I invaded her territory on a daily basis, but she would never consider being so rude as to invade mine. It came to the point that I felt I was entering a different world when I went to the laundry room, a world ruled by a raccoon and visited by a cat. During the night I was never privy to the events that went on, only to the aftermath. The sink was obviously the site of great entertainment, as water covered the floor and walls and the cat was always damp. That dripping laundry sink finally served a purpose. Raquel took great pride in climbing up and down the laundry shelves without disturbing a thing; except for the night that she lost her footing, tipping the detergent box over at just the right angle to sift into the constant drip of the faucet. The resulting bubbles and goo must have given them endless pleasure.

I actually became rather envious of Killer. Raquel allowed him into the inner circle of her world. Just because he was a cat, just because he was furry and had paws was he allowed to romp and play and share her secrets. I was too foreign, too different from what her instincts told her she should trust. The firm line between man and beast remained between us as long as we knew each other.

This was not the case with Rocky. He had long ago sold his soul for the comforts of an electric blanket and the bounty of the refrigerator. When Marie could no longer keep a yearling raccoon in her house without her parents disowning her, Rocky rejoined Raquel in her laundry room. Without a doubt, her Spartan existence was quite a shock to Rocky.

Unlike his sister, Rocky proved himself to be a social butterfly of "raccooness". Marie had spoiled him well. He was only too happy to visit with me or my house guests to perform whatever trick may be required to obtain his favorite tidbit, butterscotch candies. Raquel thought him a total fool.

Shortly after Rocky came to live with me, he talked Raquel into going exploring. One morning, very early, I heard a new type of pitter-patter under my bed. Rolling over ever so slowly, I peered off the side of the bed right into the eyes of a very nervous Raquel. Panic overcame her sense of adventure and she made a fast exit to the hallway, forgetting the stairs at the end. Bumpity, bumpity, bumpity, thump! Rocky, showing his first sense of loyalty to Raquel, followed her, bumpity, bumpity, bumpity, thump! That morning I learned that raccoons were very flexible when bouncing down a complete set of stairs for they suffered no ill effects.

I decided to close the door from then on. Not that I minded raccoons in my bedroom early in the morning, but rather I was concerned that the stairs might be the end of them.

Their second winter brought a change about them, from kittenhood to approaching raccoonhood. I realized that our interlude together was approaching an end. For all the joy that they had brought to my home I owed it to them to reinstate them in their intended native environment. The first step was to get them outside. Other than occasional outings, I had restricted their outdoor activities for fear of rabies contact. But the risk was lower, the need greater, now.

My car moved out, and the raccoons moved in, to my garage. It was a large, two-car garage, full of ladders and tools, a workbench, and odd pieces of lumber in the rafters. It was a regular raccoon gymnasium. Raquel promptly scurried up a ladder hung on the wall, across the beams and onto the lumber which hung high above where any human, dog or automobile could threaten her existence. Poor Rocky, reluctantly, but loyally, followed her up to her crow's nest. He could not understand why he couldn't just sit on his cage and eat butterscotch candies.

My visits to the garage produced a rumbling in the lumber above my head. I would then hear the shuffling of Rocky towards the ladder, which he never did master very well, as he slid rather clumsily down in his haste to procure a tidbit from my pocket. Raquel would venture out to look in disgust at Rocky's complete lack of self control, and only if I sat very still for a very long time would she come down to see what I was up to. Killer was my frequent companion on these visits and undoubtedly the reason why Raquel even considered coming down from her perch.

I would often check them just as I went to bed by shining a flashlight up to the ceiling of the garage. I met four beady little eyes gleaming back at me, assuring me that all was well in their little world.

With winter, my car missed the comforts of a garage. Finally, I decided that we were just going to have to share the space. Being very concerned about what would happen to the raccoons should they get out, I developed a routine to enter the garage as quickly as possible. I would return home, leap out with my engine idling, pull up the garage door, leap back to zip the car in, throw on the garage lights, rush back to the door to bring it back down before shutting the car off. The raccoons must have thought I was nuts. Only after a while, did it occur to me that the throwing open of the overhead door must have scared them witless, and that running down and out of the garage was the last thing that they would have considered.

Yet I remained very concerned about what would happen to my pampered raccoons should they get out in the middle of winter. Rocky knew nothing of fear toward people or dogs and would be banging on house doors for treats. While Raquel was wiser in raccoon sense, she still had little experience in the real world.

One evening, on my ritual check of the raccoons, there were no eyes peering from the ceiling, no scrambling when I unwrapped a butterscotch candy. Thinking that perhaps this was a new game, I took my life in my hands by climbing the ladder that hung on the wall. Slinging myself across the beams to where the raccoons made camp, I shone my flashlight across an astonishing mess! There, high above my workshop lay dozens of tools that had "disappeared", chewed up remains of paper, a roll of bailing twine that they were knitting into a sweater and countless other items that they had stolen up to their eerie. This, I moaned, I would deal with later. What I had wanted to find was not there; raccoons. The remainder of my search fruitless, I went to bed dreaming of Rocky peering through every windowpane in every house in Pennsylvania looking for butterscotch candies.

I started my quest early that next morning, only to be stopped by the familiar rustling above my head. There, peering down as they always had, were two sets of little eyes gleaming with the secrets from their adventure of their first night out on their own. I didn't wait for an explanation, I just slammed shut the door thankful that I hadn't found them flattened along the roadside. I left them an extra ration of butter scotches before I left for school and drove away thinking of how lucky they had been and how I had lost a night of sleep with no consideration from them at all.

My little country road was shared by only a few neighbors, all of whom used the same trash delivery as I did. It was then that I realized that this was the morning for pick-up. And pick up they were going to have to do, for my raccoons had pilfered the cans of not one, but every residence for two miles! I bet those raccoons slept like babies all day.

Living on the salary of a schoolteacher, the car I drove was a seven year old Honda Civic. I couldn't afford a nice car because I needed a truck to pull the horse trailer. I had my priorities. However, it was a great car in bad weather, often arriving home to the garage/raccoon condo loaded with snow and ice. Rocky and Raquel were fascinated by the "new" state of my car. It was enough for even shy Raquel to come tumbling down from the rafters for. All night the raccoons busied themselves with smearing the car with a mixture of melting snow and garage dirt. They climbed onto the roof and slid, time and time again, down my windshield, leaving paths of raccoon paws to blind my vision in the morning.

I would often have to stop at a service station on the way to school to have the windshield cleaned so that I could see out of it again. The service attendant was always very nice, but did once remark that perhaps I should try locking my cats out of the garage at night. What he didn't know is that I locked my raccoons IN with my car at night.

I never realized just how a Honda Civic was designed until the night that the raccoons removed all of the chrome trim from the car. It must have suddenly dawned on them that the strips of chrome, which they so dearly craved to add to their growing collection of shiny objects, were removable. A gang of car strippers in New York City couldn't have done a better job.

When I entered the garage the next morning, I tried to place what it was that didn't seem right with the car. There appeared to be grooves all around the doors and roof that weren't there before. It was my friendly service station attendant that pointed out what was wrong.

"Cat's been at it again, I see." he remarked as he scraped off a night's worth of raccoon paw prints from the windshield. "Hey, wait a minute, your trim is missing."

"Trim?"

"Yeah, it fits into this groove, but it's gone, all of it is gone!"

"Oh boy."

"Gee, just what kind of cats do you have, anyway?"

I drove off wondering just what does a raccoon do with seven feet of chrome trim.

Considering the amount of trouble it was to remove it from my car, they took it very well when I climbed up the ladder and crawled out onto the beams to retrieve the parts to my Honda Civic. It was useless to put the trim back on as long as we were to share the garage, so it was tucked safely away until I found myself raccoonless.

It wasn't long after that I failed to close the door to my car after carrying groceries to the house. The raccoons took this as an invitation to explore the wonders of the inside of a Honda. Admittedly, there is not much there, but if they had had their way, not a shiny piece of my dashboard would have remained. As it was they must have tried to remove the gearshift all night. Conceding that most of the shiny parts were permanently attached, they settled for removing the rugs and wadding them up into a big soggy wad in the back seat.

This time, I immediately recognized what was different about my car and threw a glowering glance up at those four beady eyes as I left for work in my "stripped down" Honda Civic. The service attendant was very understanding as we both worked at cleaning off the nights worth of paw prints but from the inside this time.

March came. It was early, but that unmistakable scent in the air told all that winter was waning. The raccoons could sense this. They changed. Raquel became restless, even Rocky. It took longer and longer to get Raquel to come down when I visited them. And Rocky started singing.

"Brrrr...rrrr, brrrrrrrrrr-urp! Up and down the octaves he would go, with Rachael accompanying him with a sweet little "prrrrrrrrr!. The garage offered wonderful acoustics and I would stand outside listening to their song in awe. Sometimes it would go on for over an hour, a raccoon concert welcoming spring. It was beautiful.

I knew that they needed to live in an environment where they could fulfill their intended lives, not as pets, but as wild animals. I made the decision the day I found a small, but definite, start of a hole in the garage door. It was just large enough for a raccoon paw to reach out to explore what was on the other side. They wanted out.

I spent one last evening with my companions of over a year and a half. Rocky was greedy as usual for his butterscotch candies and Raquel, to my surprise, joined us sooner than usual. I admired for the last time what beautiful creatures the raccoons were. Their fur was rich with color, from reds to deep browns, full and thick and bright. Their faces held so much expression, assisted by their "hands", which, never still, get them into so much mischief. I would miss them, but I had been so very blessed to have them share that time with me.

The next morning I loaded them into their favorite Honda heading it for a wildlife preserve where I hoped they would be able to live a full and normal life without human interference.

After spending some time picking out the right spot, I placed them in a protective thicket and opened the cage door. Raquel jumped out and never gave me a glance as she took for the woods. I had expected that. Poor Rocky, rejected by humans for the first time in his life, reluctantly followed his sister, but not without stopping to look over his shoulder at me.

I could see the confusion in his expression, "I would have been happy as a pet, so why?" "Because this is what you were meant for, not a cage, be free, be what so many of us only wish we could be."

And they were gone.

Crunchy

The first thing you should ask yourself when someone gives you a free pony is, "Why is he called "Crunchy?" Built like a tank, what he lacked in height, he made up for in bulk. My first encounter with this little demon was while giving a riding lesson at a student's home. The brother had expressed an interest in his sister's newly acquired equestrian skills, and since the parents were not too sure of his commitment, had accepted the pony from a friend of a friend. He was not the kind of pony you gave to a direct friend.

Both children were riding about the ring when I arrived, so we started our lesson right off. Crunchy seemed pleasant enough as we went through our warm up, but as soon as I asked for a trot, things started to happen. Every time Crunchy trotted to the side of the ring by the barn his rider jumped off, ran along side of him, and then remounted at a trot as they rounded the turn. At first I thought I was seeing things, but sure enough, this pattern repeated itself every time they passed the barn. When I asked for a canter, things really got trying. Crunchy took off after the other pony with his rider clinging like a burr as they cut corners and raced for the gate. There he performed the most impressive sliding stop, dumping his charge neatly on the ground. This kid was tough. He got his bearing, swung back up onto Crunchy's back and rejoined his sister. It was time to ask a few questions.

The name Crunchy was earned due to his talent of connecting knees with fences. It was usually a fence close to the barn, where Crunchy, naturally, wanted to spend all of his time. In order to preserve his knees for future use, this kid had learned to leap off at the last minute, run along side and remount, all of which he did rather well. In fact, he thought this was much more fun than riding his sister's pony, who was fairly boring by comparison. Also, Crunchy didn't canter, he only galloped, which was usually followed by a quick turn or a sudden stop. I also found him to have the amazing capacity to hold his breath for as long as it took to tighten the girth so it would always be loose when he was mounted. He hated vets, kicked when locked in a stall and flipped over in horse trailers. His past indicated that he had been given away at least eight times, that he was probably fifteen years old and that no one would take the credit for training him. Otherwise, he was a cute pony.

When the kids went to summer camp, Crunchy came to stay with me. A form of pony summer camp. I had to admit, as long as he wasn't ridden, he was a lovable little guy. I was not that dumb. But the attraction of kids to ponies came into play. In this case, it was two boys who helped around the farm. They wanted to ride in the worst way, and being that they were young teenagers, a fat pony didn't garner their interest. They were gunning for one of my horses. Since none of these horses was really suited for beginners, I told them that they would have to prove themselves by riding the pony first. Before you think poorly of me, consider the situation. It's not like I was putting a small helpless child on Crunchy. These were strong, able boys with a bit more energy than sense, and I was hoping this would teach them a good lesson. Besides, he was just a little pony, and it wasn't very far to fall

Round One: The boys have the pony saddled and Crunchy is sensing the end of his relaxing vacation. In order to show his distaste for the whole idea, Crunchy refuses to come out of the barn. Round goes to Crunchy.

Round Two: This time the boys saddle Crunchy outside. Of course, he holds his breath, and as soon as they try to mount, the saddle slides off to the side, repeatedly. Finally, the one gives the other a boost and they're off. At the first turn the saddle slides and boy meets dirt. Round goes to Crunchy.

Round Three: Things are getting tough. The one advantage the boys have over the pony is that they outnumber him. They opt to forego the saddle and ride bareback. Ever try to ride a hair covered barrel? But they've got things figured out, so one leads while the other rides. The round goes to the boys, but it wasn't much fun.

Round Four: Crunchy is ready for them. Having lost the last round, his plan is to sucker them into thinking they've won, then whammo! It works, after several trips around the pasture, they relax, Crunchy goes into his "faster than a speeding bullet" imitation with a sliding stop at the gate, depositing his rider in a heap. Round goes to Crunchy with marks of excellence.

Round Five: It's several days before the boys try again. Something about an "old baseball injury" that's causing a limp. Crunchy has returned to grazing peacefully in the pasture and is not too enthusiastic at the idea of another round. After all, he's not as young as he used to be. The boys have seen fit to seek my advice, which is a step in the right direction. Any time you can get a teenager to go to an adult for advice, you've made progress. I explain to them that a pony cannot hold his breath while running, so that if they can get the saddle secure while trotting him in hand, they will have a much better chance of staying on later. They thought that was a great idea, so off they went to the barn. It only took them forty-five minutes to catch Crunchy, twenty minutes to secure the saddle for a ride that lasted less than a minute. Crunchy ran their knees into the fence. Round is a draw.

Round Six: The boys look for a spot on the farm where there are no fences. The back yard seems to be the best bet, so, following the procedure from the day before, they step into the saddle once more. With one in the saddle and one on the ground, Crunchy has to keep up his guard. He decides to let them make the next move. The sweet smell of success has the boys congratulating each other. So far they have mastered only the walk, which is more like a poke, and being teenagers, they decide they'd like to go faster. You'd think they'd have learned from previous experience, but they've placed false hope in the saddle. Crunchy enters the trot with amazing grace and smoothness, drops his left shoulder, and comes to halt with his hoof mid sneaker. The round goes to Crunchy, again.

Round Seven: Once again the boys seek my advice. I hate to tell them too much, I'm having such a good time watching all this. I offer to give them a riding lesson on one of the horses, yet amazingly, they decline. Anyone can ride a horse, but that pony is a different story! I've taught these kids more than I'd realized and I'm proud of them for sticking to their task. So, I give them some handy tips on what to do when your mount goes out of control. They paid attention well, as that afternoon Crunchy failed to dump either one of them, even though they had some wild rides. The round goes to the boys.

Round Eight: There's more than one way to dump a kid, and Crunchy knew all two-hundred-and-ten ways. Now that both boys were able to ride both in the pasture and in my back yard, and that they were wise to the ol' knee into the fence trick, Crunchy had to think his way out of this situation. When all else fails, make the situation such that the kids wants to get off. During one of the trips around the yard, Crunchy spotted a large, and I do mean large, thorn bush. It bloomed in the spring, but now was just a mass of leaves and thorns. Little ones, but thorns nonetheless. Crunchy headed straight for it, burying his head and entire body into the mass of the bush, nothing but his tail and the face of a screaming kid to be seen. It was such a sight it took several minutes for me to get my breath back from laughing from my viewpoint in the house. I did rescue them after awhile. Round goes to Crunchy, with my respects.

Round Nine: Having decided that my yard was not a suitable place to ride a pony, the boys expanded their horizons and decided to try riding down the road, their goal being the next farm where a cute girl from their class often rode her horse. How it would look to her to see two half grown boys sharing a ride on a short, stubby pony never seemed to cross their minds. Full of anticipation, they started out. Three minutes later Crunchy came roaring up the driveway, the kid gripping the saddle with white knuckles and his face twisted in anticipation for what Crunchy planned to do with him. It turned out to be nothing. Relieved, they set out again, and once more after three minutes came roaring up the driveway. It seems Crunchy was reluctant to leave home. Each time they left, they made it a little further before Crunchy turned tail and ran. Actually, this wasn't bad fun, but it was not achieving their goal. They had to give up at dinner-time, but I knew they'd be back, and so did Crunchy. The round was a draw.

Round Ten: Crunchy had all night to ponder what to do next. Riding him on the farm was one thing, but going down the road just to impress some girl was another. After long and careful thought, Crunchy decided to put this nonsense to end. When the boys appeared the next day, he would have nothing to do with them. Try as they may, he wouldn't be caught. I couldn't help but feel sorry for them; after all, I was the cause of all this, so I offered them their original wish, a ride on two of my horses. They accepted this time and we all went for a lovely ride through the fields and woods, and I even managed to ride past their girl's farm just as she was saddling up. When I asked them how they liked the ride, they were very polite, but deep down I knew it couldn't have been as much fun as riding Crunchy.

Of Pools & Ponds

Everyone's first impression of a goat is that he'll eat any-thing that's not nailed down and butt everything that moves. This couldn't have been further from Benny's thoughts. Although powerful in his compact little pygmy body, topped off with a glorious crown of horns, Benny preferred to think of himself as a country gentleman, admiring, not eating, his surroundings. Plus he was painfully shy. Despite the fact that he had free run of the farm, for the first year or so I had him, he was rarely seen. He'd duck behind bushes or trot out of the barn at the first sight of a visitor. I decided to give him his space, yet encourage him to join me anytime he wanted. He didn't.

The arrival of Christmas also heralded the arrival of a truly original gift, Christmas geese! Not to eat of course. After 3 days in the house, and bath tub, it was unanimously agreed that geese should live in the barn. My newly acquired pair were on their honeymoon and a special stall was set up with the anticipation of yet more geese in the spring. Benny, with his usual detached interest, watched his new neighbors. Sadly, the goose died, and I was unable to replace her before the gander, Willie Wonka, decided on the life of a widower.

That spring I noticed that Benny and Willie had struck up a sort of friendship with the pony, Pepper. Where the pony grazed, so did they, when the pony came in the barn, so did they. Before long, people stopped me in the grocery store to remark on the pony and the goat and the goose threesome. We were famous. It was a good thing that the pony was quite old, for while the goat could keep up with him, the goose had to waddle the treads off his little webbed feet to keep pace. On occasion, when Pepper took it to mind to stretch his legs, Willie was forced to take to the air, protesting at the top of his lungs. Willie, despite the fact that he was a bird, was not at all fond of flying.

These three lonesome creatures, who fit nowhere else, fitted together just fine. The pony became the leader, although he could take his newfound friends or leave them. He soon discovered that leaving them behind was more trouble than it was worth, for without the

pony to guide them about the farm, Bennie and Willie would panic. The first demonstration of this was on a lovely spring day with the grass on my lawn just begging to be eaten. Pepper had devoted most of the morning to squeezing through the fence and had just started his binge in green grass when Bennie and Willie realized that their path to Pepper was barred. The bleating and honking and pacing and flapping resembled a Mummer's parade gone haywire. Despite their vocal protests, Pepper ate his way down the lawn with not even a twinge of conscience, getting further and further away, while the frantic pair became more and more distraught.

An alarm system couldn't have had a better effect on the neighborhood. I reached the back porch about the same time as the phone rang inquiring whether I was under attack. I tried to explain but the noise kept all but a shout inaudible, not to mention the stereo effect my poor neighbor was now receiving over the phone.

By the time I reached the back yard, Willie was flapping himself over the fence, leaving poor Benny, in a complete state of panic, behind. Landing was never one of Willie's strong points as he crashed into the pony, jolting him from a mouthful of delectable stolen grass and into wondering just what the heck was going on. I pulled the fence apart to let Bennie squeeze his fat little body through, taking care not to catch his horns, and the din stopped. As if nothing had happened, Pepper resumed grazing, the goat joined him and the goose set to preening his feathers. At the end of the day, I led the pony, goat and goose in procession behind him, back to his stall where they all settled happily down for the night.

They were never separated by more than a few feet from that day on. Should Pepper try one of his famous escapes, the instant alarm brought me from the house before he ever got very far. For years, I had chased down this pony at all hours of the day and night when he would escape, and now, in his twilight years, I finally found a foolproof way of knowing not only when but where, he got out. While Pepper might not have appreciated their efforts, I did.

My move to Pennsylvania did not seem to affect the threesome's attachment. My fame followed me there for having a pony, goat and goose loose in my yard. People were more worried about the goat and goose attacking them than the dogs. I suppose it never occurred to them that there were shy goats and geese in this world. Benny was so shy that when people would take pictures of the threesome, Benny was gone by the time the shutter clicked. The picture would show a shaggy black pony, a handsome grey goose and a white blur.

They came to have a fan club that visited them regularly. Quite by accident we discovered that Benny liked potato chips when a little girl flung her open bag in the air in reaction to the goose flapping his wings. His love for these salty tidbits slowly overcame his painful shyness but he still hated cameras. He was quick to produce himself every time he heard a crinkly bag , with Willie and Pepper never far behind. It was common practice to arrive at my farm with a bag of chips, stale bread and a fist full of carrots for the "guys." There wasn't a child in the area that didn't know this, saving up for a week in order to spend some time with my threesome.

One morning my neighbor called me to say. "I think your goose just crashed into our house trailer." I jumped out the door to my neighbors and sure enough, there was Willie sitting in their yard. It happened again two days later. And again. My neighbors turned out to be very tolorant people. Then one day Willie disappeared.

I searched for him for three frantic days. The goat and pony were frantic also. Expanding my territory, I drove past a farm which just happened to have a large flock of geese. One caught my eye….it was Willie! Sure enough, the farmer told me that one day a goose simply walked up his driveway and joined the flock. Being that the flock was being readied for market, Willie had not made the best of decisions.

So into a flock of perhaps fifty birds I waded, talking to Willie in hopes that he would recognize me. Not to worry, he waddled right up, took my offered treat and happily rode in the passengers seat of my car all the way home. That was the last of his flying adventures. Thank goodness.

The second winter at the new farm, Pepper gave in to old age and died quietly under his favorite tree. I watched Benny and Willie mourn for him for weeks, unable to explain to them that this was the part of life and that they would have to adjust to living without him. They never chose a substitute for Pepper, but seemed to have voted between themselves to have Benny as the leader and to continue their unique relationship. They became known as the "odd couple."

Nine years passed before I met and married the husband and moved Bennie and Willie to their third home. The husband was so excited because he had a pond and couldn't wait to see Willie's expression when he saw "real water" for the first time.

Up to then, Willie had had to satisfy his bathing needs in a kiddie pool that I set up for him every summer. He had really not given me much other choice as I was afraid he'd hurt himself trying to take a bath in the horse's water bucket, especially while I was trying to carry it. So I trotted down to the local department store and bought him a plastic kiddie pool, the kind with the fish and turtles painted on the bottom. The check out lady wanted to know if my children liked it, for she was considering one for her own. I'm not sure she believed me when I told her it was for my goose and the he just loved his pool.

He would bath and splash and honk and just have fun in the water. But he didn't like dirty water, and should I be lax, he would pace back and forth by his pool, stopping occasionally to peer disapprovingly at the mucky bottom, mumbling goose complaints under his breath. When I would dump the pool and start to refill it with clear, fresh water, he would get so excited, flapping and honking and jumping in and out of the pool until it was full. Then he'd swim as fast as he could, given a small pool, until he had a whirlpool going, then tuck up his feet and ride around and around until it stopped. Sometimes he would get swimming so fast that he spun right out of the pool, landing on his face, but jumping right up and running along side the pool, and hop right back in. I loved his pool too.

The husband, eager to win Willie's confidence, thought that if a pool was fun, a pond was better. He would tell Willie all about the pond while feeding him stale bread. Willie would munch away in awed silence. Then moving day came and we pulled the trailer right to the edge of the pond so that Willie would see it as the first thing

29

in his new home. He and Benny had been nervous in the trailer and were anxious to hop out. The husband, camera in hand, released them, hoping to capture the high point in a goose's life.

Benny took one look at the camera and did his disappearing act. Willie, to the husband's delight took one look at that pond and started to run. Wings outstretched, head held high and honking like a runaway train, Willie hit real water, and for the first time in his life started to swim. He swam here, and there, and everywhere, honking his pleasure to the world. Everyone was so happy and excited that no one noticed Benny peer out from under the trailer to see what was going on. Forgetting his fear of cameras, he bolted towards Willie only to find that geese can do something that goats can't. Swim.

This was too much. Furious that Willie would leave him stranded on high ground, Benny raced back and forth along the bank bleating his lungs out. "Get back here! What do you think you're doing out there! How could you do this to me, I'm all alone"! Poor Willie, just as he found what he'd been looking for all his life, he had to give it up, for a goat. He never seemed to question why Bennie couldn't join him, he just knew he wouldn't.

The secret pact they had made nine years earlier bound them to be together and together they would stay. Willie made several attempts to get back in the pond over the next few weeks, but Benny wouldn't have it. The husband made every effort to try to work this out for him, but the bond was too close, the pond was off limits, period. Reluctantly, the husband bought Willie a kiddie pool, placed near the pond, where he bathed regularly and dreamt about his day on the pond, with his goat grazing watchfully by.

Second Drawer Down
on the Right

When Mabel dropped into my life, she taught me just how unprepared I was for dealing with a weasel despite having cats and dogs and geese and horses and chickens and ducks. She was none of these. She was a FERRET! And since I was a push over for cute furry animals, Mabel made easy work of me.

My first mistake was to give her the run of the house, like a cat, something that I really don't recommend if you want to remain in control of your personal property. Mabel moved into my typing desk, the second drawer on the right in the winter with her summer residence being my bedroom closet. Like clockwork, she would move herself from place to place with the expectation that I would concede each territory and respect her love of naps, right to acquire objects loved by ferrets and provide maid service. And I did.

The closet offered an interesting (ferret wise) collection of shoes and sneakers. Fitting in a sneaker is not easy, even for a ferret, and such an act needs to be respected. I soon learned that I was obtuse to ferret etiquette when it came to choosing which shoes I was going to wear in the morning. Grabbing a shoe encased ferret resulted in an explosion of brown fur followed a severe scolding in ferret-speak which lasted longer than I really thought necessary. Hey, people make mistakes!

The discovery that her winter living quarters was to be in the second drawer on the right in my desk was a bit unnerving. I only used the desk when I had to type something, which was as infrequent as I could possibly make it. I only type because my handwriting is so awful. My typing is not much better, but it is still easier to read my restrikes than my script.

I was typing away when I ran out of White Out. My search through the desk brought me to open the second drawer on the right and there, staring me right in the eye, was a ferret. Remembering that I had been in the drawers the day before, I thought I had inadvertently locked her in there and there she had been, poor thing, until I just by luck opened the drawer again.

Overwhelmed with guilt, I took her to the kitchen for some "extra milk" and satisfied that she was none the worse from the experience, returned to typing. Several hours, and bottles of White Out, later, I again opened the second drawer on the right, and there, staring me right in the eye was a ferret. Humm. Since I had only one ferret, I knew that this was not coincidence.

"Okay", I muttered, "what are you doing in the second drawer on the right"?

"I live here!"

"Oh." Remembering our confrontations over the shoes in the closet, I really didn't want to bring up my feelings about her entitlement to "Squatter's Rights" so I conceded the deed to the second drawer on the right and started to move my things out.

"Just what do you think you're doing"? she chirped angrily.

"Taking my things."

"They stay with the property, it's in the contract."

"Oh."

I could see that this was going the way of the sneakers in the closet and that I was pathetically

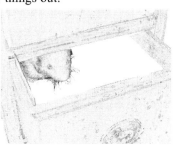

not aware of ferret protocol yet again. The "things" happened to be the carbons to all of my paid farm bills. While I may not have needed them right then, I would come April 15, so I planned to make a raid sometime before that when Mabel was "out". Unfortunately, the next time I checked on the second drawer on the right Mabel had shredded the bills to form a wonderfully cozy little nest. I wondered how my accountant was going to take this. I still dream of being audited by the IRS and presenting them with a plastic bag stuffed full of the shredded bills from 1982, ferret hair and all.

If I thought I had lost on proprietorships of the sneakers and the second drawer on the right of my desk, I was to soon learn that ferrets know no bounds. What they perceive as "theirs" is no longer "yours', period. Sharing is not in their vocabulary. The next items to become part of the Ferret Kingdom were the insoles to every set of muck boots I owned. Every set.

My first task of the morning was to feed the horses. But first I needed to retrieve the insoles to my muck boots from the second drawer of the desk, where Mabel hoarded her prized collection. My daily invasion and removal of two of these fascinating objects sent her into a fuming frenzy of chirps and chattering. While I methodically trod to the barn to feed and sweep and muck about, Mabel paced furiously at the door for my return.

I was greeted with "it's about time and what do you think you're doing with my insoles."

While I tried to pacify her with "morning milk", which she had to share with three starving cats, (remember that "share" thing, she didn't think that was funny either) she never took her eyes off of my feet.

The removal of the boots sent her into action as soon as my foot was clear. She would pop into the boot, emerging triumphantly with the insole clenched in her teeth. Sometimes the tricky little pad would get stuck, which gave Mabel considerable grief and me considerable entertainment. She would drag the boot to a chair or table leg on which it became caught and from which the insole could then be pried free to the continuous chattering of ferret foul language.

Then came the tedious trip from the kitchen, across the living room, through the "window pane that was not there in the door because I had a ferret" and into my study. The "windowpane that was not there" was my compromise with her which gave her access and me privacy by way of a glass paned door.

Getting through the "window pane that was not there" with an insole half again as long as she and clenched in her teeth sometimes proved a problem. It tripped her up unless held perfectly at an angle, but this angle made the leap through the door a lucky event at best. Sometimes the problem resulted in repeated bashing against the door, which raised Mabel's ferret foul language to a new level

"Chirp, chuurp, chitter-chitter chuuuurp"! (interpretation "why does my human have to have such darn big feet!)

Once through "the windowpane that was not there", she slithered and writhed under the desk, up behind the first drawer and popped into the second drawer, exhausted, but elated to have "saved" one of her insoles. Then she tore back to the kitchen to get the other one.

When Mabel wasn't dragging insoles around the house, she was sleeping. She considered her rest very important and viewed any interruptions as glaringly rude behavior on my part. The vacuum cleaner was "Public Enemy #1" when it came to her beauty sleep. I was not exactly "Susie Homemaker" but I did notice that if I didn't vacuum the rugs now and again, people made remarks. Of course none of these remarks ever came from my horse friends because they understood that a clean barn was more important than vacuumed rugs, but every so often a non-horse person would somehow slip into my house and I had to be prepared. They didn't give a hoot that my feed troughs were scrubbed and that the hay was neatly stacked and the horse's tails were brushed and fluffy, they only cared about

vacuumed rugs. I tried to explain this to Mabel, but she didn't give a hoot about a clean barn or vacuumed rugs, all she cared about was her drawer full of insoles and uninterrupted naps.

No matter where Mabel was napping at the time, she would come roaring into the living room whenever I was vacuuming the only rug in the house. It was a big living room and a big rug. Furious that I was once again disrupting her naps with that awful "thing", especially since she had told me not to do it again after the last time, Mabel turned on the machine in full fury. As I pushed it forward, Mabel would leap backwards, chirping ferret obscenity after ferret obscenity. Then, as I pulled the machine towards me, she would launch her little body in the air, landing inches from the whirring brushes, snarling and snapping in full offense. Of course, I would have to push the machine forward again, she would retreat, then as I pulled it back, she would leap.

Push, retreat, chirp, pull, leap, snarl. Back and forth we'd go, all around the living room. Donna Reed never had to put up with this. When my guilt finally got the best of me, I turned the "thing" off and put it away. Watching me was my exhausted but triumphant little ferret, pleased that I finally realized the errors of my ways and put "Public Enemy #1" away for good. She would then shuffle off to resume her nap leaving me to ponder how I could clean the rug without using a vacuum.

While the vacuum cleaner made Mabel furious, the typewriter, which occupied the top level in her desk, made her a total wreck. This was a manual typewriter, you know, the kind that you had to actually push the key against the paper which made an odd little click sound? Probably a valued antique today, but at that time in my life, it was the only show in town. Those nasty little clicks worked on Mabel's nerves like Chinese water torture. Then there was the carriage return that went "slam-dunk" at the end of every line sending shock waves right down through to the second drawer on the right. I could hear her rustling about in the shredded bills as I worked. After every "slam-dunk" came a pitiful little "chirp". It wasn't long before she appeared, fixing me with that beady little stare of hers. I couldn't really blame her, I hated typing too.

Unable to nap, she would shuffle out of her drawer to retreat to a more peaceful location to continue her nap. Sometimes that was the couch, actually between the cushions on the couch, which meant that unless I carefully inspected the same every time I wanted to sit there I took the chance of sitting on, and really upsetting, my ferret. Again.

While I never quite succeeded in kitty litter training Mabel, she did learn to use paper. Of course, that meant any paper and one was well advised not to leave important documents or homework lying around the house.

Ferrets are not affectionate in the way cats and dogs are, but they do have their moments. Periodically, I would wake up in the morning to find a ferret curled up in bed with me, happily sharing another nap. While play sessions were rare after her"kittenhood", she would on occasion offer the best of entertainment by playing with me, preferring "pounce on the human's foot from under the couch" to "chase the rubber ball".

Her best moments were in her fondness of rolling in clean laundry right as it came out of the dryer. Static cling would cause my panties to stick to her furry little body as she'd race about the house shaking them off.

She thought me a funny type of creature and while she had me pretty well trained, I'm sure she was glad that there was only one of me. We really got along quite well after a fashion. I didn't bother her and she let me live in the house.

Harried by a Screen Door

After decades of feline companionship, I have learned that no two cats are alike. Such an understatement when it came to Dirty Harry and Killer McKenzie. During the period of time that I shared my life with them I came to learn that no two cats could be more different.

Killer McKensize was a gray taunt bundle of muscle with a hint of jaguar in his gait. He took life very seriously in regard to cat business. Trees were to climb, mice were to be stalked and birds to be chased. Killer was, in his opinion, the equivalent of a big game hunter. Handsome, cunning, looking for a fight and never around when you wanted him. He rode into town only long enough to have a quick meal before heading out again. We had a provisional relationship.

Harry, on the other hand, was a mass of hair guided by serene yellow eyes and followed by a graceful plume of a tail. Life was his oyster and he took everything with calm reflection.

Harry had been conveniently left behind in my truck at a horse show. The sneaky kid who dumped him there, also by the name of Harry, claimed to be the offspring of a close friend of mine. Neither she, nor I, believed that he was. Just what I needed was a kitten at a hot, dirty horse show. Neither of the Harrys seemed at all concerned with my feelings. Harry, the cat, came home with me and lived happily ever after. Harry, the kid, grew up somehow, somewhere.

Harry, the cat, earned his surname "Dirty" because he was. On a hot summer day, Harry's favorite spot was the kitchen sink. It didn't matter to him that I wanted to use it.

"Hey Harry, will you move for crying out loud, I want to use the sink"!

"Yeah, yeah, can't you go somewhere else, I just got settled in here"! Oh, he reminded me of his namesake!

He liked anything that had water in it, sinks, toilets, ponds, buckets, dog dishes. He was not picky. Rain puddles were OK too. He would sit out in the barnyard side by side with my ducks and goose in a rain storm as the water rolled down their backs. His long, raccoon like coat was reduced to the look of a weasel when wet, but he didn't care. If you are a wet longhaired cat, you are also a dirty, wet, longhaired cat. Hence, Dirty Harry. Despite his name, Harry was a gentle soul and never once picked a fight just to "make his day".

"Morning milk" was a ritual all of the cats in my household, but for Harry, enough was never enough. One hot, lazy summer day I was drinking a wonderfully refreshing milk shake and enjoying a good novel. I sipped away unaware of the presence of a milk stalking cat. His timing was just right to get a few licks from the glass between my sips. He managed to get the lion's share of the milkshake before the contents reached the critical point at which a cats face was no longer going to fit. Not accepting this, he pushed his face in hard, hard enough to get his head stuck. His attempts to paw free were unsuccessful. Confused, he picked up his head with the glass, and milk shake, stuck to his cheeks. When the liquid sloshed into his face, Harry panicked straight into the wall. This got my attention. I saw before me a very unhappy cat, a drowning, unhappy cat. I snatched the glass from his pinched and blubbering face. It was a fate no cat would want to bear. "Here Lies Harry, Drowned in a Milkshake!"

Harry was no dummy. From that point on, he never got stuck in another glass. Instead, he learned to use his paw. Dip, lick, dip, lick, Harry could polish off a glass of milk, right to the bottom. He expanded his paw talent to foods other than milk, thoroughly enjoying cleaning out the remains of a spaghetti sauce jar with his paw. He looked a tad pink for a day or so, but he didn't seem to care and spaghetti became one of his favorite dishes. He preferred to slowly suck each strand into his mouth just like a little kid.

Being a rather large cat, Harry had no trouble´stretching to his full height to see what was served at the table. If he liked what he saw, a simple tap with his paw was cue enough for me to start dropping tid-bits his way. If I were slow to figure this out, Harry would very politely remind me every two minutes or so that he was still patiently, obediently waiting on the floor slowly starving to death. He was a regular at meals.

The only time Harry had a problem was in a car. He didn't get wild or leap on my face, he got sick. It started the moment we got in the car, "Meow."

Then I'd start the engine, "Oh-wow-meow," drool.

As I pulled out the drive, "No-wow-meow-wow," drool, gag.

By the time I got to the vet he was a cross-eyed, greenish yellow cat with drool down his normally pristine white front. Everyone in the waiting room was convinced he had rabies. As a matter of good business, my vet let us in through the side door after that first visit.

Harry's claim to fame was the screen door in the kitchen. Whether it was his size or his ability to use his paws, he had mastered the spring mechanism and could come and go as he pleased in the summer. This beleaguered Killer as he lacked Harry's technique to master that door.

Every time Harry placed his full length up against the door, Killer was right behind him. As the spring latch gave, Harry would slide his body into the yawning crack, with Killer snugly behind him. At just the right moment, Harry would leap through to the beckoning day beyond.

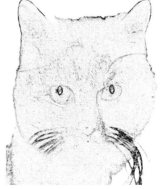

Killer was only a cat's whisker behind him, but it just wasn't enough. SMACK!, Killer's face became imprinted in the screen and his whiskers would become a fraction shorter, again. Frustrated and mortified, Killer would utter a most pitiful "meow" for me to open the door. That wretched, insolent, bothersome door.

Considering Killer's high opinion of himself, this was very hard for him to take. On the other hand, Harry never seemed to notice. As the summer progressed, this little scenario would repeat itself several times an hour. Harry would let himself out in order to check the weather, and, if it wasn't quite right, would return through the door by plucking at the screen until he popped open the spring latch, sliding himself neatly through the opening. Killer never made it in either. He was "Harried" by a screen door!

Harry's ticket in and out of the house gave him a freedom that Killer coveted in a way only a big game hunter cat could. Try as he might, he simply could not produce the same result with that screen door. I offered to open the door for him, but it just wasn't the same. Killer was not a happy cat.

Then a miracle happened. I had to leave the cats on their own for five days while competing with my horses in Kentucky. I didn't wish to leave them locked in the house, returning to two cats wild with cabin fever and five times the USDA recommended amount of dirty kitty litter for houses my size. Nor did I wish to leave them locked out only to return to find poor Harry locked between the screen door and the main door in his attempt to get in. I decided instead to remove the screen from the bathroom window. Instant cat door!

Terribly pleased with my solution I brought each cat up to the bathroom to show him his new path to independence. Once out onto the roof, they could choose between an inviting evergreen tree or the laundry pole to get to ground. Cool. While Harry took this all in stride, Killer was ecstatic. Finally, freedom!

My return five days later was greeted by two happy cats. While I was sure they missed me, they would have missed the couch, cat dish and toilet bowl even more had it not been for the window. To show their appreciation, Killer charged right up the laundry pole, onto the roof through the bathroom window, galloped down the stairs and greeted me inside before I could put my bag down. Oh, how he must have used that window while I was gone! But so did several hundred flies.

First order of business was the replacement of the screen. Five minutes later I heard a crash in the bathroom. I rushed up the stairs to find Killer picking himself up, blinking, then hopping onto the sink for his next bound through his window. Crash, again. More screen prints on his face. How could this nice friendly window have changed to be another nasty screen? Killer tried one more time, putting everything he had into it. Another crash. I felt so sorry for him as he gave that window one long last stare before he stalked downstairs. Harry sat indolently by, washing his paws and wondering when all of this ruckus would end.

It wasn't long before my return home became old news to Harry so he stretched himself up against the screen door. Just as it always had done before, the spring latch popped, Harry stuck his paws and head through the crack and, slick as Houdini, he was gone. Only this time Killer was not right behind him. Instead he pretended that he didn't have any interest in following Harry for one of their outdoor adventures that day, or any other day for that matter. Killer had decided that screens, in any form, were too fickle to trust and that Harry could have his door.

Christmas Goose

Never did it occur to me that I would have one goose for over half of my life. What started out as a fun little adventure has turned into a life long experience with a bird with an individual personality. Who ever thought geese had personalities?

Willie Wonka arrived on Christmas; Christmas goose! After losing his mate, he attached himself to my goat, Benny, and busied himself about the farm in an unobtrusive way. They were pals, the goat and goose, so when Benny died, Willie took it hard. It was then that the husband learned the truth about geese, that they could live up to thirty years. I could see in his face that he hadn't planned on that, nor had he planned on getting another goat. But we did.

Goatee deserves a standing ovation for his short, but entertaining life with us. I had heard that if I bottle raised a baby, that they would be more like a dog than a goat. The husband reminds me that I should not take to heart everything I hear. It was great fun bottle raising a baby goat, they are so cute and climb into your lap and follow you about. Too bad they get big.

The German Shepards probably had more to do with making Goatee doglike than the bottle. He would race through the barn with them, banking off of walls and leaping over wheelbarrels, Shepards at his heals. The barn help loved that. Perhaps that was the base of my suspicion that the barn help did not always treat my baby goat with the tenderest of care.

The sense of humor that developed in this goat was stupendous. He was cunning, daring and downright comical. His first discovered delight was in hopping on parked cars, bouncing from rooftop to rooftop, until one day someone left their sunroof open. Goatee had eaten most of the contents of a purse before we discovered him missing.

One morning I discovered a car in our pasture. Cars appeared in our pasture from time to time, usually after an all night party at the neighbors. Sometimes it is hard to distinguish the main road from a pasture. I call the local cops and let them handle it.

Right about the time the officers threw our somewhat uncoopertive guest against the barn wall to arrest him, I noticed that they had left the door to their cruiser open. Then I saw the head of a goat appear behind the driver's wheel. Oh, boy. Look at all of those wires! Oh, boy, Goatee was going to have the best time in there. I can't tell you how difficult it is to interrupt two officers reading off the Miranda Rights to tell them that their cruiser was under attack by a goat, but they did thank me after a fashion. The damage was minimal....whew!

I remained in the minority when it came to loving Goatee. He delighted in pushing over little children and butting unsuspecting dogs against the wall, creating a richochet effect with their little bodies. People were catorigized as friend or foe. Friend meant that you showed up with bags of goat goodies which you offered as payment for the right to cross the parking lot to the barn undisturbed. Foe meant that you forgot the goodies. One boarder turned back after driving half way to the barn because he realized that he had forgotten the goat food. He was no fool.

When we moved to Vermont, I doubt that any of the boarders missed Goatee. But he missed them. Vermont was quiet, peaceful and just us. Except for the builders. We had to build a barn and do considerable remodeling to the house and outbuildings, activities that would keep Goatee entertained for months.

Builders proved more of a challenge than boarders, but it was with them that Goatee rose to his full glory of goatness. As a line of defense I offered the builders squirt guns. Goats hate water, and they hate water squirted in their face even more. On each tool belt, there hung a hammer, screwdrivers, gloves and a squirt gun.

It came to be that just seeing that squirt gun was enough to cause a goat retreat. Except with the new guys. My builders did not lack a sense of humor. Every new guy that came on the job somehow missed the goat tutorial. Goatee made short work of them The new guy usually ended up on top of the pick-up truck trying to eat his lunch while his buddies ate undisturbed.

Goatee liked following the builders around but at a safe distance. Once in while he got lucky and could grab a box of electrical supplies, spewing them along the ground as he ran. One job required a man to go up and down a ladder, repeatedly. Goatee was faithfully at the bottom each time the man came down. Concerned, I asked if I should lock him up. "No, no", said the man, it being a matter of pride that one was not afraid of the goat, "he's fine."

Goatee must have been there an hour formulating his plan. Finally, as the man came off of the ladder, Goatee reached up and untied the bow that held the tool belt. Plop. Tools everywhere. He was good.

Goatee liked children. He would run right up to them and knock them over then watch as they squirmed around to get up before he would knock them down again. He never butted them, just knocked them over. So, to protect my friends two year old, we placed her in a stroller while working with the horses in the barn. Suddenly, the stroller flew by us with Gaylyn whooping her lungs out as the goat pushed the stroller, and her, through the barn and up the drive at considerable speed. She thought it was great, wanted him to do it again.

Willie stayed at Goatees side faithfully when he got sick and was truly distraught when Goatee was gone. The husband's repeated statement that there would be no more goats, melted right on the spot. He went right out to find another one, but there were none to be had. He came home instead with another goose.

Willie had not seen another goose in over twenty years. It was a big shock. The husband, expecting instant gratification from the goose instead got a stony stare, "what the heck is this, I wanted a goat!". Two days of being locked in the barn together produced tolerence of each other, at best.

We had named the goose "Girlfrien' " and offered her every goose comfort we could think of. When we thought they had settled down, we opened up the barn again. Girlfrien' immediately set wing for home, home being two miles down the road. Oops. Although Willie had shown absolutely no interest in his new partner up till then, he set up a din of honking and flapping that would wake the dead. The poor husband, being the responsible party for not getting a goat in the first place then bringing home a goose that now has left poor Willie is such a state, offered to retrieve Girlfrien'. Poor guy.

Girlfrien' had not managed to make it back to her former home, but had been sighted swimming in another neighbors pond. It was a big pond. The husband was in the process of dragging a boat to the water's edge when she took wing again. Not wanting to loose her, he took off on foot, chasing her down the stream bed for over a mile, then losing her. Wet, tired, covered with mud, he came to his senses. No more goats. No more geese.

I had just settled Willie down when my neighbor called to tell me that a goose matching the description of Girlfrien' was in her apple orchard. Great. I jumped in my truck. Sure enough, I found a very tired goose trying to fly out over the eight foot deer fence surrounding the orchard. Getting in had been a lot easier than getting out.

Picking up a twenty pound goose can be hazardous. Once you have the wings pinned, one is best advised not to let them go. Knowing this, getting into the truck with a goose in my arms called for some creative manuveurs. Once in, I had no choice but to turn her loose. It was while driving the short trip home that I discovered that geese can too fly inside of a truck.

Willie greeted Girlfrien' as the long lost love of his life. They honked and billed and waddled about as if they had done so all of their lives. Go figure. The husband once again lost his resolve about goats and geese and now we had not one, but two geese and eventually another goat. I wondered at what point he will realize that this replacement process will be endless?

At twenty-six, Willie was kinda slow but Girlfrien' adjusted her pace to his as they strolled about the farm looking for good things to eat. The husband decided that if you can't beat 'em, join 'em, and become quite the fan of Girlfrien'.

While Willie was a connoisseur of apples and carrots Girlfrien' preferred only lettuce. Not spinach, not celery leaves, but lettuce. Early on she figured out that the lettuce came from the tack room refrigerator, which was also full of apples and carrots which held no interest to her. She liked to follow me into the tack room and sit in front of the refrigerator, begging.

Every night I called Willie into his housing by saying "night, night, don't let the coyotes bite". My house sitters found this rather amusing. One rather capable young man simply was not going to reduce himself to saying "night-night" to a goose, thank you very much. After two nights of chasing the geese all over in order to put them in their quarters, he succumbed. 'Night-night" and poof, they went in. His recount of this episode at the local lunch spot brought roars of laughter from his friends. They too had tried other methods of collecting my creatures, but had also resolved themselves to the fact that the goose knew only one way to go to bed, and that was to say, "night-night!" If it has worked for twenty-six years, don't fix it!

The Perfect Winter Ride

You don't run a horse boarding business, it runs you. If I ever had a free minute while at the stable, it was instantly filled. But the time I took to spend with my boarders, and their children, produced some of the best part of my day.

An overnight snowfall decked the landscape with crystal and white. The kids were off from school, so naturally, they were at the barn. At a loss as to what to do with themselves, they were driving me crazy. Finally I suggested a ride.

"In the snow?"

"Isn't it too cold to ride a horse?"

"Can I ride bareback so I stay warm?"

"Won't that itch?"

"Can you make us hot chocolate when we get back?"

They liked the idea.

As the kids collected their mounts, the husband was gesturing frantically from the tack room. "Are you nuts?" he popped. "There are twenty-five mile per hour winds out there. The wind chill factor is minus twelve!" It was hard to refute a man who takes his weather seriously. I was remembering careless gallops through snowdrifts when I was a child. We never noticed how cold it was because we were too busy having fun. "Be a sport, we'll bundle up", I held.

Our little troop looked a far cry from the photos taken last summer at the local shows. Hard hats were hung with scarves, making everyone a foot taller. Orange, green and hot pink boots replaced the more traditional kind usually worn around horses. Shaggy, unpulled manes danced around Mohawk bridle paths and the white ponies were anything but white.

Choosing a trail that just the day before had been deep in mud, we trotted merrily up through the woods, emerging a the top of the hill at exactly the spot where my husband's weather friends had measured the wind chill factor.

Within the three-minute period that it took the crest the hill, Mitchell's' ears turned a color I'd never seen before and Katie's pony's slobber, left over from her last apple, froze into icicles. The husband was trying desperately to say "I told you so" but the wind kept blowing his mouth shut.

But I was still entranced by the snow and the prospect of reliving a childhood memory. Picking up a trot, I encouraged my little group by telling them that posting would warm them up.

Once over the hill, we found protection from the wind in the valley. The snow-covered dirt road offered perfect footing for the horses – and a quick lesson on the differences between a shod and unshod horse.

Clipping along behind a shod horse puts you in direct fire of snowballs formed under pressure into deadly ice missiles with a trajectory deviously aimed at your head. An unshod horse can't counter-attack as the snowballs fall harmlessly from the hoof.

The husband's big hunter was shod. Simply through size of stride, she offered the most firepower and was to be avoided. Except by Katie's little twelve hand pony.

Wise in her twenty years of experience, she found the perfect spot in which the missiles flew harmlessly over her fuzzy little head. Katie, on the other hand, had to duck some of the lower ones, which she did with increasing glee.

Finding the perfect pace in such weather is not easy. A trot needs to be fast enough to keep warm by posting, but not so fast as to break a sweat on the horse. I had visions of hot chocolate by the fire at the end of this ride, not wrapping hot horses in coolers.

Trying to keep the pack at an appropriate pace was not easy as the missile war was in full engagement. We had traveled three miles by the time we got to a hill again.

We stood as a group at the bottom of the hill, staring reluctantly at the blue sky beyond the crest of the hill. The wind was in full force up there-and it looked COLD.

"If we do this at a gallop, it'll be over before you know it", I yelled.

They were with me. Hitting the crest of that hill at speed was like jumping into a mountain stream without testing the water first. The lee side of the hill was boring in comparison, but my rosy-cheeked riders were grinning at having experienced that hill.

Heading home, the horses naturally picked up their pace. The sooner they got rid of these crazy two-legged creatures upon their back, the sooner they could relax in their nice cozy barn, chewing on some hay, stopping only occasionally to sip some water.

Charging to the head of the pack was the geriatric equine with short, but fast, legs complete with child clutching gamely to the reins. To Katie's rescue came the big strided missile launcher. As the husband blasted by me, I could hear the thuds and grunts of those behind me on whom missiles found their targets.

Once the pony was under control, our ride home was pleasant and relaxing. The horses had but a mere hint of a sweat, so we were soon beside the fire sipping hot chocolate amid a discarded but appreciated pile of warm clothing.

The husband couldn't refrain from tuning in the weather channel. "The wind chill factor made today one of the coldest days yet this winter, a good day to stay indoors," said the weatherman. One look around at my rosy cheeked group was proof that he was wrong. It was a perfect day for a winter ride.

Fred of the Farm

There are barn cats and there are house cats. It is not for me to decide which is which, the cats do that themselves. Miss Marple went from a barn cat to a house cat in the time it took to drive her home. Poof, princess. Fred, on the other hand, decided on the barn.

The barn was not at all a bad place to live if you were a cat. There was a hayloft full of mice, a comfy couch in the tack room and a constant supply of humans to pet, feed and cuddle a cat. Fred was no dummy.

One of five abandoned kittens, Fred had the windfall of being raised by a Golden Retriever. His mannerisms reflected the smiling, tail-wagging greeting of my generous dog. The dog would swagger up to a person, jump up with a paw on either side of your head and "give a hug". So would Fred. He was a very cool cat.

We had other barn cats, but Fred stood out. Fred was the cat that sat with us while we watched a rider take a lesson, the cat that followed us out to the pasture to catch a pony, the cat that everyone stroked while talking on the phone and was the only one brave enough to ride in the goat cart. Even the horses knew Fred as a friend. They would reach down with their soft muzzles and Fred purred quietly to them. He was welcome to share in the warmth of their stalls where they carefully stepped around the curled up orange ball of fur.

Fred's fame went beyond the barn. The little girl down the road tried to trade with the husband two of her kittens for Fred. No deal. So when Fred turned up missing, we were upset.

Fred had been missing once before. He liked riding in cars and it seems he was doing some car exploration the day he first disappeared. A boarder's wife, having taken the car on errands the next day, stopped at the local garage because the car was making strange noises. The strange noises turned out to be Fred in the trunk. He was returned with the sincerest of apologies.

But his time Fred was gone. Everyone checked their car trunks; no Fred. We contacted the blacksmith, the meter reader, the telephone company, the oil delivery driver; anyone who could have driven a vehicle to the barn and mistakenly taken off with Fred. Nothing.

Over a month had gone by when I spotted a thin ginger cat walking down our drive. The cat had a determined step, not hesitating at any distraction as he approached the barn. I thought it just another stray until the cat swaggered up to me, put a paw on either side of my head and "gave a hug". Fred was back!

Fred never again got into a car.

Instead he opted to ride in my pony cart. Rolling along through the barnyard and out to ring, Fred would sit like a dog on the seat next to me. At first I was nervous that he would jump out, but it soon became obvious that Fred was very content in his perch.

Many a time, in the company of Fred, I exercised the pony through the fields surrounding the farm with no apparent distress from my companion. He would sniff the wind and blink with obvious contentment at being chauffeured about in such a way.

Upon our return, Fred would genteelly step down, stretch, and proceed to saunter into the barn for a bite to eat under the full gaze of the other cats. They must have thought him pretty special to get service like that. He was.

Pickles and Ponies

Matching a child to a pony can be tougher than running a dating service. Every time I'm sure that I've made a big mistake, the intuitive powers of animals and children humble me, again

The appearance of little girls at our boarding barn was inevitable. Our boarders had children and as those children grew up, the pony question became more and more serious. My little Welsh pony was a delight with little children and earned the title of baby sitter, but that was all she ever intended to be. She was not in the least bit interested in jumping over fences or galloping around pastures. It was obvious that, in Katie's case, she needed a more suitable pony.

So-Fat arrived at Christmas. She had hair like a yak, was fat as a cow and had a disposition to match. She divided her time between eating and rolling in the mud, making her "white" coat appear like a giant powder puff. Katie cried when she first saw her. "She's fat and ugly!" spouted the kid. Her parents looked at me horrified. "Give it time," I told them, "these things have a way of working out."

By spring, we were still working things out. So-Fat was a self-declared queen of the pasture and gave anyone wishing to put a halter on her a vigorous workout before allowing herself to be apprehended. This cut down on Katie's riding time considerably. Matter of fact, the pony never made it to the barn most of the time, and when she did, it was with an exhausted kid. Smart pony.

When we did manage to collect "herself" from the pasture, it was with a sulky creature in hand. Once saddled, So-Fat's idea of being ridden was a browsing walk between mouthfuls of grass. The appearance of a crop resulted in scurried little runs between mouthfuls of grass that were not acceptable to Katie's nervous system. My attempts to explain to Katie that this seemingly monstrous beast had carried many a youngster to ribbons at shows and was truly a wonderful child's mount fell on deaf ears. Even her parents were beginning to think that I had fallen on my head one time too many. "Give it time," I told them, "these things have a way of working out."

I decided that I had better try to help things along by working with

So-Fat when Katie wasn't around. All ponies have their selling out price when it comes to goodies, but it was obvious that So-Fat was holding out for the highest bid. Nothing I tried worked to catch her. She just laughed at a can of grain, pinned her ears at a peppermint, danced around me for carrots and sneered at horse cookies. I was finally able to get my hands on her when she decided I had spent a reasonable time running around the pasture. By the time I scraped the mud and shedding hair from her, I had more of a workout than she did. I was beginning to sympathize with the kid.

I felt pretty silly trying to sit on a fifty inch pony with a full sized saddle. The look on her face the first time I tried it told me that she felt it was an equally ludicrous idea. Ponies are for children, and I was about to make an unforgivable transgression. Luck would have it that she was trained to drive. How hard could that be? Our first trip out, she backed the cart right into the husband's Volvo despite my pleading, yelling or whacking her insulated little fat furry body with a whip. Clearly, I was no match for her, she had been seasoned by children.

Back to the kid. Finally, So-Fat was content to trot around the ring with Katie as long as the gate was closed. I tried to make this important little detail clear to Katie's parents, but perhaps I wasn't graphic enough about what could happen. At the first opportunity, So-Fat did the distance from the ring in to the barn door in Olympic time. Thankfully the barn door was closed. Otherwise Katie would have found herself careening down the barn aisle and into a stall, but she connected with that possible scenario rather quickly and her interest in riding waned.

In a last attempt to make this work, I lured Katie back to the stable by offering her a cart ride. I didn't tell her who I was hooking to the cart. Despite her look of apprehension, the presence of an adult while in range of the little whirlwind gave Katie some muster. Game kid.

Off we went. My driving experiences with So-Fat had improved considerably since the Volvo incident, so I was rather confident of our little venture. We actually were having a good time right up to the point when the dog ran out from behind an ornamental bush.

The voice and whip are important method of communications to a driving animal, but So-Fat was not receiving any messages. Once again, she completely ignored my voice and the whip and was on a flight path of her own. Our saving grace was a row of rubber garbage cans that cushioned most of the impact. We came to rest in a neat little pile.

I was about to concede that my ability to choose equines for little girls had slipped some when I heard Katie's voice.

"Poor little So-Fat," cooed Katie as we hopped out of the cart to run a damage report. "Did that nasty dog scare you?"

Personally, I had no argument with the dog, but I was calculating just how many cans of dog food I could get from that pony.

"Do you think that you hurt her with the whip?" she asked me, the big dumb adult who was still shaking the adrenaline out of her fingers.

Katie hadn't seemed to notice that we had been traveling at the speed of light dragging an ornamental bush through someone's back yard only minutes before. All she cared about was So-Fat's feelings. She had her arms wrapped around the pony's neck with just enough room left for me to see a wise old eye peering back at me. "Mind your own business, things have a way of working out."

Every day from that point on, Katie and So-Fat were together. They drove the cart down the road, they galloped across fields, they jumped over logs, they did all the things that a pony and a little girl could do to be happy. When they had a problem, they worked it out themselves. My "services" were no longer required, thank you.

"What happened?", asked her parents.

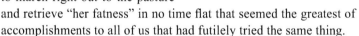

"Ponies and children have their own little world," I tried to explain as if I understood it. "Once they find that there's a need for each other, nothing is impossible."

However, it was Katie's ability to march right out to the pasture and retrieve "her fatness" in no time flat that seemed the greatest of accomplishments to all of us that had futilely tried the same thing.

Unable to contain myself any longer I finally queried, "So what's your secret, Katie?"

"Pickles!" she grinned

I would have never thought of pickles. Only a child could do that. I knew that they must share many other secrets that were none of my business. As I watched them gallop off through the field I realized that I had known all the time that things would work themselves out.

A Day at the Races

It's October. The air is crisp, the foliage a rainbow of colors and the social event of the year in Far Hills, New Jersey is a day at the races. Every one, and I mean every one, goes. Tents are pitched, caterers are brought in and on Sunday morning every tailgate in every station wagon is dropped to produce a picnic fantasy.

The competition is stiff. Ice sculptures, tuxedoed waiters and fountains of champagne. But fancy as they are, we are the show-stoppers. We arrive in horse-drawn carriages.

Our assembly is quite impressive. Four-in-hands, pairs and singles turned out in the finest sporting carriage to celebrate the day. Since we are the "attraction", we are escorted to the infield of the steeplechase course where races will be run later in the day. After the fifth race, we will parade before the crowd before leaving. Until then, we could picnic and chat with the race goers. It really is a lovely way to pass an autumn day.

The husband and I were each driving a pair of Morgan horses, mine being quite green and this being their first public outing. I had two very capable friends riding with me in the carriage, Olivia and her husband Rudy.

Such outings with carriages are very social. Like a moving party. The bigger the carriage, the bigger the party. The horses seem to understand that once we have stopped, there is no need to do much more than cock a leg and take a nap. They have been to these parties before, no rush to leave.

Rudy was standing by the horses' heads, chatting with friends. I was balancing a plate full of gourmet goodies in one hand and the reins in the other. We were just settling into our lunch as the grounds prepared for the first race.

"They're off!

From our carriages, we could easily see the horses start the course and progress over each jump. Steeple chasing is a very old sport. The horses race a turf course while negotiating hurdles up to three feet in height. It's very exciting to watch, as each hurdle can change the place of the field and it is only the boldest and fastest horse that wins.

At the third hurdle, my near (left) horse, Beau, suddenly developed a keen interest in steeple chasing. My off (right) horse was still napping. As the field raced by, Beau's nervous system blew a circuit and he lit up like a Christmas tree.

He knew, deep down in his heart, that he wanted to be a steeplechase horse too. He did not care that a)he was attached to a carriage, b)another horse was attached to him, and c) he didn't know the first thing about steeple chasing.

By now, the other horse was wondering what was so wrong with Beau and was considering disconnecting her herself from him as quickly as possible. To anyone that drives, this is known as a "situation". I had been in situations before and knew that this one could go from bad to worse very easily. Throwing my half-eaten plate of food to the wind, I made the decision to not wait around for the fifth race. It was time for us to make an exit.

Unfortunately, the exit off the infield was in the same direction that the field of horses had last been seen. Convinced that he was truly going to get a crack at joining them, Beau displayed considerable enthusiasm at heading in that direction. His pair mate, still wondering what this was all about, decided to join him in his fervor. I had my hands full.

A wired pair of horses is nothing to take lightly. While I had them under control, I had them just under control. I was pulling against the force of not one, but two powerful horses, and they were pulling against me. It's not brute force that controls horses, rather a series of communicative tugs on the reins, tugs that mean something to the horse. You hope. Sometimes, like this time, they just can't seem to concentrate on what you are saying to them, kind of like controlling a young child on Christmas morning. Good luck.

I was hoping that the quarter mile or so through the parking complex would settle them. Not so. Olivia's husband muttered something about my biceps and trapezoids and not wanting to meet me in a dark alley. I knew he meant that as a compliment, but I was wondering if my arms could be pulled out of their sockets by creatures outweighing me two hundred to one.

I could picture me a year from now, driving with the reins in my toes as people quietly asked what happened to me.

"Oh, she had her arms ripped out one day at the races. Kept the horses in control though, heck of a horsewoman."

The exit way from the parking lot was an under pass which merged to a traffic light on a major highway. It afforded little room for an unsuspecting motorist going sixty miles per hour to react to a horse drawn vehicle going seven miles per hour.

The entranceway, however, offered a clear view of the highway right to the traffic light. If I timed it right, I could scoot across without having to stop. Stopping, so it seemed, was not an option. So, I went for the entranceway, ignoring all of the "wrong way" signs posted along the drive. I was committed to my plan when the police car swung off the highway heading right for us.

Olivia didn't see him at first because she was wondering if my blouse seam was going to split up my back and cause us further embarrassment. The cruiser drove up to us, the cop rolled down his window and he leaned out and said with authority,

"Pull over! "

"Pull over?" It seemed so ridiculous that I repeated what he said. "Right", the cop demanded. "Pull over!"

The horses weren't at all interested in pulling anything but my arms out. My failure to "pull over" caused the officer considerable distress. He put his car in reverse, matching the speed of the horses, who I had finally reduced to a slow bouncy trot, to make his next demand.

"Just what do you think you are doing?

I couldn't answer that; I was so focused on keeping us alive. Olivia saved me by outlining our plan.

We were informed that we could not, and would not, be able to continue our route as we were violating countless rules of the road. No doubt we were. The horses remained at their slow, bouncy trot with no intention of going any slower. He leaned out and said with authority,

"Stop!"

I heard Rudy snicker.

"I am very sorry officer," I tried to explain, "but this is the closest I can get to a stop,"

"Then turn around", demanded the officer.

That was not an option either. The curb was too high and the road too narrow to negotiate a turn in a carriage pulled by two bouncing horses. I could see we were really upsetting this guy, his face was getting redder and redder.

"Sorry, again", I replied. We were halfway to the light by now.

Fuming at our blatant disrespect for his badge, his shiny black and white cruiser and his oath to protect civilians, he blustered,

"If you insist on continuing, I am going to give you a ticket!"

Taken aback by his demeanor, Olivia could not restrain herself. "A ticket? What are you going to write on it? 1901 Studebaker, two-horse power with failing brakes going the wrong way out of a parking lot?

We started to giggle.

Seeing that this was going nowhere, he exercised good judgment for the first time since he opened his mouth; he left.

We hit the light just in time to cross on the green. Under the admiring eyes of motorists on the highway, we looked like the vision of tranquility.

"Oh look dear, there goes one of the Amish buggies out for a Sunday drive!"

Two miles down the road the pair forgot what it was that they were in such a rush about and relaxed into a lovely trot that carried us all the way back to our waiting horse trailer. My arms remained in their sockets and the day ended on a pleasant note.

We had a great story to relate to our friends when they rejoined us after the races. They all agreed that getting the ticket would have been great fun at traffic court.

Take Care
the Names of Cats

There can never be enough cats in my day.

If I can get a cat's attention, I consider that a compliment. Using the right name is important. There is a lot in a name and cats know it. They want it to roll off of your tongue as if you are addressing royalty. HRH Queen Elizabeth would no more respond to "Hey Liz" than a cat respond to "Kitty". Because of this I have always taken great care in the naming of cats. There was Ron-Ron (Purr in French), Attila the Hun-gry, Cat-A-Pillar, Kitty Carlyle, Velcro, Maybeline (the Queen) and Miss Marple.

The most interesting name was "Strubble Peter". I won him as a prize at an endurance ride in Puxatawny, Pennsylvania. When I went up for my award, I was given a choice between a ribbon or a tiny black and white kitten who looked a little young to be there without his mother. I proved once again that I was a sucker for furry little animals.

The little black and white kitten was not at all happy about his new circumstances. He mewed at the top of his lungs from inside a bucket while we struggled to finish packing for the trip home. The acoustics of that bucket were amazing.

Once in the truck, he perched himself on my friend's chest and settled in. As long as she didn't move, he was happy. We didn't have any kitten food so we shared our dinner by chewing up tiny pieces of chicken, which we fed to him kind of like a baby bird. It did not appear that he had much knowledge of solid food. We finally stopped at a grocery store for some baby cereal and milk. That he liked, dipping his entire body into the goo while he sucked it up. It was a long trip home

When I unpacked the truck, I presented the husband with a big box and said, "surprise". Staring up at him was a tiny cereal covered black and white ball of fur protesting bitterly at the top of his lungs.

"What is it?, he replied.

"It's a kitten! Isn't he cute!"

Fact is, he was a mess.

"He's kinda young, isn't he?" questioned the husband.

"Well, yes, but we'll just raise him until he can be on his own."

"We?"

Back in Pennsylvania Dutch Country where the husband grew up, one cannot help but pick up some of the local sayings. Such as, "Feeling rouchy". That means that you can't sit still, like in Church. Or, "getting all frahutteled". That means, "flustered". When your hair is a mess, people say it's all "strubbly".

The husband named him "Strubbly".

Other than my carrying him around in a fanny pack for two weeks until he was large enough and confident enough to go off on his own, Strubbly had a normal kittenhood. And even after my vet warned me that pre-weaned kittens don't always grow up as normal, we think he did.

Having grown into a most handsome longhaired cat, he was my pride and joy. So, naturally, I worked him into our dinner conversation during a cruise in the Galapagos Islands. To our surprise, the pleasant little Swiss woman who barely spoke English perked up at his name.

""Strubbly," she said, "you mean Strubble Peter?"

We didn't have a clue who Strubble Peter was, but were eager to find out.

Strubble Peter is a Swiss character, not unlike Charlie Brown's Pigpen. His fairy tale is told to children so that they understand the ramifications of not combing one's hair or caring for one's nails. Strubble Peter was a walking mess.

Until this point, we had not connected how the term "strubbly" had come to Pennsylvania. But the Pennsylvania Dutch had trav-

eled through Switzerland on their way from Germany to the United States, and had obviously picked up some of the local slang. They adopted the word "strubbly" from Strubble Peter's higgledy-piggledy appearance. It took a trip to Ecuador to find this out!

So Strubble Peter tried on his new name and liked it.

I can't remember ever being able to use the bathroom alone since I've had cats. The attraction is universal among them, head for the lou, guaranteed you will have company. I've tried closing the door; it just results in a paw jutting under the door and a lot of scratching.

While the toilet is fun and the sink can be interesting, it's the bathtub that holds my cat's attention. The bathtub seemed a logical place to throw the cats some catnip from time to time. They would paw and roll and lolly-gag around, emerging with silly cat grins. The husband refers to the bathtub as the opium den. It followed that the cats would sit in the tub waiting for some good time feelings.

Any human entrance into the bathroom would result in the movement of the shower curtain. This gave rise to a pounce against the curtain from the inside of the tub by a cat-nipped cat. Should any other cats be standing by, they would pounce from the outside of the tub. The curtain would swish wildly as in each cats turn, they would defend their position. Sometimes the cat would perch on the tub between the two curtains. While this offered better pouncing power, it also meant that the cat could be pushed back into the tub. Thud.

This game, which started with Kitty Carlisle who taught it to Strubble Peter who taught it to Miss Marple who taught it to Bob (simple, but it fits, he's a Manx) who taught it to me, makes visits to the bathroom longer than normal. It appears that they like having a human join them in their game. I long ago learned to use a comb or a toothbrush to tickle the curtain as the cats are not always aware of their claw power. Tickle, tickle, pounce, jab, pounce, jab, thud. I have to admit it's a lot of fun.

Strubbly has the most incredible instinct for hunting. Having missed the kitten tutorial from his mother, he acts purely on instinct. He can flatten himself to the ground and stalk for hours his prey. Comfortable with the bathtub as they are, Strubble Peter found yet another use for it. A place to store his prey until he sees fit to finish it off. Blithely stepping into the shower stark naked to find yourself eye to eye with a wet, leaping live mouse is just one of the many pleasures of living with cats.

Kitty Carlisle was raised as a classic Jeweled American Pussycat. Her mother, Maybeline the Queen, taught her everything she needed to know about being a Princess. She slept on the softest bed, ate with a pickiest appetite and never went out in bad weather. Should I open the door to a rainy day, she would turn on her head away. She would then go to another door, perhaps thinking that this one would offer better weather. Only after seeing the other side of every door in the house would she give up the thought of going outside and opt for the couch.

Her uncat-like behavior of burying herself under bed sheets, clothing and rugs resulted in more than one surprise for the cats, dogs and humans that lived with her. Tunneling her way in, she would lay there for hours thinking herself invisible. Until you stepped on her. When she taught this little maneuver to our miniature dachshund puppy, we had no choice but to take up the rugs.

Our bed is a canopy style one, with a broad cornice completely surrounding it. It is a particularly enticing place for cats. Kitty Carlisle mastered the top of the bed by jumping to a chair, hopping on the dresser, then leaping to the cornice. The entire bed would shake as she walked around four feet above our sleeping heads. Strubble Peter who was a good two pounds heavier than she would join her. This aerie provided an ideal place to watch the birds at the feeder outside our window. The birds arrived around dawn.

Kitty Carlisle particularly liked that cornice. I would find her curled up on the tiny space of the corner post sound asleep high above the bed. Or swinging her paw at my head as I attempted to pull down the covers.

The cat's only way down was onto the mattress below. And us. Like a cinder block dropping from the sky they would land. Boom! Boom! Off to the bathtub to check on the catnip while we repositioned ourselves to get back to sleep. Ah, cats.

The Toy Box

My attempts to calm the ferret over my infraction of moving her toy box to allow me to paint her corner of the closet was not going well. I was not sure if it was the language barrier or her tendency to be bull headed that was causing the problem. I realized my transgression shortly into the project, a task that would have been much easier had I relegated Dulcinea to her cage, but it being a slow winter day, I was up for some entertainment. I was getting more than I bargained for!

Ferrets operate under a code of behavior that they assume you know about when acquiring them. Being very gregarious in nature, they cannot fathom why anyone would go out of their way to annoy them. Far from being needy, the few pleasures they have in life are sacred, and I had stepped over that line.

While she had a cage she spent only nighttime in it. During the day she had free roam of the bedroom, bathroom and walk-in closet. Ferret paradise. She did have other quarters in the basement, a huge wire cage with "two stories" of ferret playthings such as a ramp, a hammock, a hanging bell and a box with her second favorite sweater in it. Her favorite sweater resided in the closet. Her cage was dubbed "the ferreterrium" and she spent time there only when I was away.

I actually felt guilty that Dulcinea did not have the run of the house as my past ferrets had. Her fetish for digging out plants from their pots, however, precluded that idea. I had toyed with the idea of fencing in the garden so that she could help me with that chore, but had not yet perfected a ferret proof enclosure. Pet that she might be, I knew that she would return to the wild given the opportunity.

I also had the problem of one cat. The other three were no problem at all, but Strubble Pete" had had his fill of bull headed ferret behavior and was not about to move from his comfy spot on the bed where the sun shone just right just because she thought he should. The result had been a fur flying, spit and hissing contest which left the bed strewn with cat hair, ferret fur and a little blood. Neither seemed willing to back off so I intervened. The feud never died, with both eyeing each other up each time they found themselves in the same room. For the sake of peace, Dulcinea was asked to concede and spend part of the day in the closet. The closet was the size of a kitchen, but she still felt put out.

Because she didn't have the freedom of the house, Dulcinea didn't have many friends. She had me of course, but I was a bit wanting to a furry critter. Fur, it seemed, was a great attraction to Dulcinea, as demonstrated by her reaction to the presence of a baby goat in the bedroom for a few months one spring. She loved rubbing against his legs, not necessarily loved back by the goat.

She did luck out in having Oaf, the cat, grow up with her. He was a kitten, she was a kit, so not knowing any better they became friends. He started out being called Little Black Job (LBJ) but grew and grew and grew into a twenty four pound black long haired cat with minimal athletic ability. Hence the name. Twenty four pounds of cat making a tactical error when jumping up onto a chair is memorable. He seemed to have adopted the ferret code of behavior in that he slept most of the time with periodic trips to the feed dish. In that, Dulcinea had a buddy and they often napped together.

Since ferrets spend most of their day asleep, and all of the night asleep, where they sleep is very important. Hence the need for a favorite sweater. Hers was on the top shelf of the husband's collection of sweaters. Under the ferret code of behavior, the husband was not to consider wearing that sweater, to which he conceded once she explained it to him. The explanation was an explosion of ferret noises as she clung to the sweater while he attempted to put it on. He complained he was bitten, but she claimed self-defense. She has a tiny little mouth, how bad could it have been?

Once the top shelf of the sweater collection was secure, Dulcinea sought out secondary and tertiary sleeping quarters, just for a change of pace. Under the coverlet in the middle of the bed was a favorite. As was the towel shelf. Despite my efforts to build her a very cool box with tunnels made of mailing tubes it took years before she considered it worthy to sleep in. I was so touched when she finally did.

Sharing a room with a ferret took some adjustment. At times, I felt as if I was living in a Harry Potter movie as periodically the waste paper basket would start dancing, or the bedclothes would rumple and bump or shoes would disappear. Crossing the room in bare feet with a ferret in pursuit was not as easy as one would have thought. Socks are highly recommended!

During her "kitten hood", I plied her with all kinds of toys that pet stores assured me that ferrets would love. What ferrets love, more than any toy on earth, is an accessible roll of toilet paper. Safe for days, sometimes weeks, the toilet paper repeatedly succumbed to periodic attacks by the little weasel. A new roll, property shredded, can fill the average sized bath room. In absence of toilet paper, she preferred the cat toys. Especially the fuzz covered balls with bells in them. Chewing the fuzz off was so much fun. The now naked ball could be chewed into a crumpled up semblance of a ball and carried about in the mouth.

These balls somehow found their way into the box spring of our bed. Perhaps a tiny hole in the cover invited them in. Any movement in the bed resulted in bells ringing which while entertaining for a time, became rather annoying in the middle of the night, especially to the husband. Finding a ferret-proof cover was not that hard. What was not easy was removing those belled balls!

Dulcinea's toy box was of her own invention. No longer able to store her treasures in the box spring, Dulcinea set out looking for a new location. In my determination to housebreak her, I had numerous litter boxes set about the bedroom, bathroom and closet. My rationale was that she would always be near a box should she need one. I hadn't figured on the ferret code of behavior which dictated having a favorite box and no other. One of these boxes was triangular in shape, sold to me by the pet store with assurances that ferrets loved triangular litter boxes. Never used, the empty box was shoved into the far corner of the closet, under a rack full of shirts and well hidden from view. Perfect place for toys.

Into the box went all of Dulcinea's possessions. The stripped-down-crumpled-up-belled-balls of course. Followed by select insoles from my sneakers and boots (this obviously dictated from the ferret code of behavior as my previous ferret also loved insoles), stolen toothbrushes, several cat toys and a flashlight. The flashlight was the kind I used when riding in the dark on endurance rides and must have been snatched from my bag when I was not looking. Ferret modifications made it rather worthless to me on a trail ride, but it was a treasure to Dulcinea. Treasures, according to the ferret code of behavior, were not to be touched.

I discovered the toy box by accident. My watch went missing and one morning I heard a beeping such as one hears when the alarm goes off. On my hands and knees I bushwhacked through the hanging shirts to come upon the stash! Retrieving my watch, I could not but help to take a look at what else was kept there. It was only moments before a frantic ferret jumped into the corner and began dancing about, chirping and squeaking at my transgression. Having heard this all before, I backed off, but insisted on keeping my watch.

It was gone the next day. I would not have minded letting Dulcinea keep my watch had it not been for the condition of the balls and the flashlight. Thinking it safe hanging from a hook near my bathroom mirror, Dulcinea proved me wrong. I finally secured it in a drawer.

Dulcinea was fastidious when it came to keeping her toys. Out one would come to be played with or slept with depending on her mood. But back it would go once done. The only period of time that the toys stayed out was when I was confined to a hospital bed after a serious riding accident. Dulcinea was delighted to have yet another bed in the room and often spent her days with me, asleep of course.

Sleeping with a ferret is not as easy as it sounds. They don't stay asleep. They nap, toddle off for a bite to eat, swing by the bathroom sink for a drink, return for a longer nap, pop out from the covers for a look see, return to the nap, discover your foot and take a sample bite, react with indignation at your reaction to the sample bite, show you what a real bite would feel like, scurry about under the covers while you attempt to catch them because of the biting, follow you to the dresser and watch you put on a pair of socks, follow you back into bed, nap, check out the foot with the sock, take a sample bite of the sock, react with indignation at the lack of reaction to the sample bite, bite harder, give up on that, take another nap, pop out from the covers and lick your face with a teeny weenie soft tongue, toddle off for another snack, bring some of that snack back into bed, react with indignation at your reaction to rolling over onto that snack, scurry off of the bed to retrieve the bits of snack you just brushed from the sheets, return to the bed with the snack, noisily finish off the snack being sure to leave tiny grit-like crumbs, settle down for a well deserved nap, wake up refreshed, pick out a stripped-down-crumpled-up-belled-ball from the toy box in the closet and roll it about under the bed, grow bored with that, settle down for another nap with the belled ball, react with indignation when you roll over on the ball, react with even more indignation when placed into the cage for the remainder of the night.

My confinement to a bed lasted longer than I would have liked, but Dulcinea loved it. She thought so much of this that she started to move her toys into the bed with us, including the treasured flashlight. She meant it as a compliment and I took it as such.

I meant to return the compliment by showing a friend the toy box. I realized my mistake when demonstrating what happened when a toy was removed. In this case I chose the flashlight for after all, how many ferrets had a flashlight?

I put it on the bed after which a ferocious ferret clenched it in her teeth with the intent of getting it back to it's proper place as quickly as possible. Not calculated was that the flashlight weighed more than the ferret. Two hard tugs brought her to the edge of the bed and the third tumbled her and the flashlight to the floor. Lots of chirping. With increased determination, she picked up that flashlight in her teeth and dashed into the forest of shirts, my friend dying of laughter and wanting to see that again. No way!

So, there I was, trying to paint the closet and appease a ferret at the same time. Toys were flying about the room being stashed frantically here and there after the cover of the shirts had disappeared. My attempts to explain that this would be a temporary situation were worthless to an animal that had no concept of time. Now was now and measures had to be taken.

Retribution was being handed out in the form of hiding my sponge. Much lighter than a flashlight, it traveled well from the closet to the bedroom. Looking at the clock, I realized that this project should have been done hours ago had I simply locked up the little darling. But then what would I have done that slow winter day for entertainment?

Don't Light a Match

Among the top ten nastiest animal smells in the world lies Dachshund breath. It's right in there between camel burps and fresh kitten poop. Dachshunds are famous for this as verified in any Dachshund manual you may pick up, "Start early. Get your puppy used to you putting your fingers in their mouth and rubbing their gums a couple of times per day. Buy a small dog toothbrush and gently run it inside the cheek pouch next to the molars and around the sharp 'spiky' canine teeth. As the puppy gets older, twice a week use animal toothpaste with a properly sized brush." The manual ends by saying, "good luck."

Anyone with a sixth grade level of reading comprehension should have picked up on the "sharp 'spiky' canine teeth." One needed a young vet with lightening quick reflects to clean a Dachshunds teeth. I recall one vet who produced an itty-bitty muzzle with the thought that it would facilitate a rather delicate examination of my Dachshunds hinder region. How she got it off is anyone's guess but she was wise to muzzles forever. Not that muzzles are very helpful in cleaning teeth.

We did our best as pet owners. The husband firmly grasping the dog while I danced around trying to get a shot at the plaque that plagued her mouth. I had about a thirty per cent success rate. It came to the point where we had to spell to each other when contemplating another mouth attack. Even with that, simply stepping within 5 feet of the cabinet where the dreaded dental pick lived was enough to send the Dachshund hiding. In other words, it was a loosing battle.

By the time the Dachshund reached her senior years her breath was as lethal as tear gas. Periodically, when we simply could not take it any more, we hauled her to our vet who warned us that the only way he was going near that mouth was if she was under the influence of drugs. At her age, this could have killed her but we didn't care, she smelled dead already.

It had been some time since the Dachshunds last trip to the vet when I took her along on a five-day trip to New Jersey with my horses. I also took along my friend, Jenny, as she was good company and our horses loved each other. Jenny and I had a great time riding, the horses had a great time being together. The only down side of the trip was when the Dachshund yawned.

On the way home, we visited for the night with old friends in Pensylvannia. I should have known the invitation was a set up as she just "happened to have" a litter of kittens. Jenny was of no help so we found ourselves northbound on the New York Thruway with two horses, one old Dachshund and four freshly weaned kittens. It turned into a memorable trip.

We had tucked our little bundles into a dog crate in the back seat of the truck. Home being eight hours away, Jenny could not contain herself and convinced me to let out one, just one, kitty at time. It will help socialize them, she quipped. First kitty was a roly-poly orange tabby that Jenny immediately named "Pumpkin Head". Jenny was very original when it came to names.

He was delighted with his freedom and climbed all over Jenny before discovering me. Exhausted from his romping, he nestled contently into my neck, just behind where the seat belt crossed my shoulder, and fell asleep. This led Jenny into wanting another kitty for her to play with and, to stop her whining, I granted her request. This one was a cute little tabby girl who purred and rolled and frolicked until she too sought out a nice comfy place for a nap. On top of my head.

This delighted Jenny and before I could say anything she had the other two on her lap. Couldn't leave one behind in that nasty old kennel, could we? These two proved quite lively and were sliding across the dashboard when I realized I was approaching a tollbooth. There simply was not enough time or anywhere to pull over so into the "Get Card Here" lane I went.

Tollbooth collectors never seem to notice what is going on inside a vehicle and this one was no exception. I suppose being exposed to an endless stream of nondescript faces makes one numb to something different. We were different all right. I could not lower the window beyond a crack for fear of a kitty springing out onto the thruway nor could I turn my head without dislodging the kitty on my head. Jenny was so busy trying to scoop up the kitties on the dashboard that she was of little help.

Surprisingly, a toll card pushed its way through the open slit of the window and we were able to proceeded on. I half expected to be pulled over by a patrol car after it received a call from the tollbooth operator about someone trying to drive with a cat on her head. It was illegal to talk on a cell phone while driving in NY state, why not extend that to playing with kitties while operating a motor vehicle? But either the tollbooth operator didn't notice or she was a cat lover.

Realizing that we soon had to refuel, we collected up kitties from all over the truck before stopping. I cared for the truck and Jenny cared for the horses. Innocently, I pulled open the driver's side door to get back in and was swept back by a billowing lime green cloud that seared through the lining of my sinus and left me gasping for air. You guessed it, one, perhaps all, of the kittens had added a second top ten nasty animal smell to the very small confines of my closed up truck.

Reflecting back, it was a good thing I did open the truck door when I did before the noxious fumes inside blew out a window. Jenny swears that the two people refueling at the nearby pumps staggered back also. We had a situation on our hands.

We decided to pull the truck to the far side of the station in order to not risk having the fire department called in by some customer who might mistake our lime green cloud for a gas leak. First order was to remove the Dachshund who, upon closer inspection, was given credit for at least fifty per cent of the situation. The other half was contributed to the back of the kennel where the kitties, after holding "it" up until we pulled into the station, gave it their all.

An hour later, and thanks to the station owner for letting us borrow the hose, we were back on the road. It still wasn't pretty inside the truck, the upholstery having absorbed more of the odor than one would think possible. Or perhaps it was our clothes? Either way, it would have been dangerous to light a match. Even Jenny agreed that it was a wise decision to leave the kitties in the kennel lest one feel the call to nature again.

When I rolled down the window to pay our toll we did notice the toll collector step back for a second, but true to form, took the money, handed me a receipt and looked to the next vehicle. But I would bet she washed her hands before the next car.

Getting Nudged

Why, after having goats over half of my life, had it never occurred to me to have a house-goat? It would be a lot easier, and a lot more fun, to bottle raise a baby goat in the house, rather than the barn. The notion of a house goat had never crossed the husband's mind either. This oversight was corrected with the acquisition of Nudge.

After twenty years together, the husband had learned a few things about me. On the occasion of watching television, and actually watching a commercial, we would view the image of a man presenting a woman with a tiny, beautifully wrapped present. The woman, discovering a sparkling diamond anniversary ring, would throw herself at her man.

"Don't ever, ever, do that to me," I would comment. A diamond ring was about as useful to me as a third leg. I had a trunk full of family jewelry, lovely stuff, which scared me to death to wear. After all, I had managed to bend my wedding ring, knock a diamond out of my engagement ring, and several other nice pieces, much to the horror of our jeweler who was doing his best to stay one step ahead of me. He thought the rings were antiques when actually they were purchased new. "What do you do all day?" he would mutter. "Don't ask" would return the husband, rather frustrated in his attempt to shower me with jewels.

"Not to worry dear, I know better," the husband would respond. The man was smart enough to know that presenting me with a tiny motherless kitten or a flea ridden, wormy, stray dog or a renegade horse would mean so much more than some dumb diamond ring. So he knew that his suggestion of shopping for a baby goat would be met with loving arms.

Since our last goat earned favor by not jumping on cars, the husband was led to believe that all Cashmere goats did not jump on cars. He was expounding on this fact while we stood in a snow-studded pasture at the foot of Streaked Mountain in Maine viewing the spring crop. The breeder, a very sweet man, kept wanting to correct this conception of goats, but caught my eye in time to realize that it was best to allow the husband to hold that thought. After all, he did want to sell us a goat.

I had learned long ago that it was best to let the husband pick our goats. It tempered any future accusations about whose goat just ate the tulips. Presented with seven tiny goatlings to choose from, it was a formidable task. Bouncing around in joyful innocence, none sensed the seriousness of the moment. One was to come home with us to live a pampered life while the rest were to remain in the herd to produce wool and meat for the farm. We always picked a buckling for that reason.

The husband took his time. The little guys, but five days old, already showed personalities as they played in the barnyard. After a full hour of goat entertainment he picked the buckling that I also had silently chosen.

Since his mother had produced quadruplets that spring, missing one was hardly upsetting to her. Nudge seemed to sense that his lot in life was one better than his siblings and barely noticed the transition from barn to car. Or it could have been the simple fact that in early April, the car was nice and warm. Without a backward glance, Nudge settled into my lap for the long ride home and his new life.

Since the timing of getting our new buckling was rather rushed, we had not completely thought it through. Being early spring, it was still pretty cold out for a lone buckling in the barn, and since he was settled so nicely in my lap, the husband felt that perhaps we should stop and pick up a playpen for the first night or so. No argument from me. But who was he kidding, once that buckling made it into the house, he was staying.

Into the parking lot of one huge "everything under the roof" store we went. I goat-sat while the husband perused the aisles for, in his own words, the cheapest play pen he could find. The clerk, somewhat taken back by this kept suggesting a better quality product for his little darling grandchild. "Darling?" quipped the husband, "this one has cloven feet and horns!". It was only when the clerk looked like she was going to bolt and run did the husband confess that the recipient of the playpen was none other than a five day old goatling. The entire sales staff walked the product out to our car for a look see!

The responsibilities of being a surrogate goat mother were dictated to us by Nudge. Never were we to leave him alone, nor were we to be late with his milk bottle. Non-compliance with either rule brought about an outburst of goat panic. We trained very quickly. So, have goat, will travel. Riding in the car he loved. He went

to meetings, dinners, horse events and neighborly visits. I would pass him to whomever, and he would curl up in their lap and enjoy the proceedings. Right from the start, he became very socialized. Once in his playpen, he slept the night through. He did, however, need to be right next to the bed, and my middle-of-the-night trip to the lou somewhat concerned him. His own trips to the lou, a spreading of sawdust off the back herb garden, were governed by how often we thought about it, which was not quite often enough. But for a barn animal, he did amazingly well with the hygiene thing.

Bottle time was always a high point in Nudge's day. He gave me ten seconds after the microwave dinged to get that bottle to his lips. He would accept his bottle from anyone, which proved a big hit with houseguests and visitors. With six bottles a day everyone got lots of practice. The bubbles left on his mouth when he finally sucked that bottle dry earned him the nickname "Sugar Lips", a term of endearment he still holds today. It truly was sad when, three months later, Nudge and I shared the pleasure of his last bottle.

During this time Nudge did his best to teach me to speak goat. He had a full vocabulary, which he used constantly. "Maah?", "nat", "mmmmmaaat", "mmmmm", "blah", "poof". I tried my best to keep up with him, but my attempts were met with a confused look as if I had just said something pretty stupid. Eventually we settled on a few key "words" that we both understood. "Maatt!" which meant bad goat. "Mmmmaaa" which meant good goat. I felt it best to keep it simple.

The cats were not so amused by the new addition to the household, but Dolcinea the ferret was. Peering through the mesh of the playpen, she would scurry from one end to the other trying to figure out just what was inside. Finally a trip over the side deposited her at Nudge's flank into which she buried herself much to his surprise. "Blah," he went. Scared her right out of the playpen.

Somehow that first encounter melded a friendship between ferret and goatling. While attempting to brush my teeth I was often joined by both. They just loved the sink It made my personal hygiene a challenge, but it was worth it for the chuckles.

Soon I was aware that they had worked out a little game between them, a mix between hide and seek and soccer. Dulcinea kept her collection of toys in a little box in the corner of the closet. Where else does a ferret keep things? Out of this box she would produce her toy of choice for the day, usually a ball with a bell in it. It is much more fun if one's toy jingles. Nudge would join her in playing with the ball but soon it was obvious that Dulcinea was not into sharing.

Eventually, both ball and ferret would disappear into the closet resulting in Nudge butting into the husband's hanging shirts until the ferret was found. Out came a mad ferret, jumping at the legs of the goatling. Goatlings hate that. As the game escalated, it became apparent that they were both having the time of their lives. The only harm was to the husband's shirts, but he didn't have to know.

As Nudge grew and became more agile, the ferret game moved to new levels - onto the toilet and eventually into, of course, the sink. Most memorable was Dulcinea being picked up by her tail and wildly dangling over the sink while I choked on toothpaste laughing.

On the cuteness meter, goatlings score a Ten. If anyone should figure out how to freeze a goatlings growth at this time, everyone would have one. For two months our constant companion was a tottering little ten pound, eighteen inch goat who would sleep at our feet at the computer or curl up in his antique wingback chair during dinner. He nuzzled us with affection and sighed when he was content. Even the horses thought he was cute! I would relive those two months again any time.

As Nudge grew, so did his ability to get into things. Gone were the days of his fitting into his chair. Gone were the mornings he was willing to sleep in. And endangered was most of our furniture from the attack of goat hoofs. I found myself saying "maat!" constantly. But it was leaping from the floor into the stove where three pies were cooling that convinced me that Nudge needed to move to the barn. I managed to fix the pies so that the little hoofprints didn't show so much and everyone accepted the excuse that I had dropped them. Although I do think the husband was suspicious.

To the barn Nudge went; not that it was so bad a place, but different indeed from having one's own chair and playing in a sink. He screamed bloody murder. This resulted in a phone call from my neighbors, who lived half a mile away, to see if someone was torturing the goat. I was reminded that Mrs. Dugdale was on the zoning commission and that perhaps there was an ordinance against such things. I explained the situation, but she still seemed to think that surely there was a better solution. Easy for her to say.

Eventually Nudge settled into life in the barn, but never quite forgot where the house was. Every chance he got, he charged through the porch door for a whirlwind visit chased by me, if he was lucky, or the husband if he was not. It is amazing how much damage a goat can do in a short period of time.

But one day the door must not have been secured after we left and Nudge let himself in. Imagine his joy! To be able to leap onto countertops, eat bananas and drink from the sink without that constantly annoying "MAATT!" in his ears. Eventually bored, he managed to stuff himself into his chair as we found him quite asleep when we returned home. It was then that I realized how much I missed having him in the house.

It's not like we ignored Nudge after he moved to the barn. During that summer we spent a lot of time with the horses and working around the farm. Nudge helped us put up new fencing which would have taken half the time had it not been for his antics. He once bit through a tape measure the husband was using. He just walked up to the stretched out tape and "chomp" it was two pieces. How cute is that!

Since he loved to ride in a car, it followed that he would love to ride in our 4 wheel drive "mule". I would buzz around the farm, even over to the neighbors, with Nudge on the seat next to me. Sometimes the dogs would join me, and a jostling for the best space would ensue, the goat, understandably winning the best spot. However, one determined pooch, To Be, was not at all deterred by some goat and would sit herself on top of him. I was left with barely enough hiney space to drive the darn thing.

The most amazing thing was that Nudge did not, as predicted by the husband, jump on cars. He bounded in and out of the beds of pick up trucks, into tractor seats, onto a bulldozer, all over horse trailers, with the hay bins a favorite, but never on cars. Who would have thought?

Had it not been for a prominent member of our hunt and his wife telling the husband stories about their house-goat, Nudge might have remained in the barn. But learning that such an animal lived in what would be considered a normal, well-adjusted household, was the turning point for the husband. Naturally, I invited these wonderful folks to dinner.

Their goat lived in the house when their son was born. Concerned for the child's safety, they placed tennis balls on the goat's horns. The child, now in his twenties, still has memories of being knocked down and stood upon by said goat. He laughs. His parents laugh. I laugh. The husband was wondering if anyone we know is normal.

To the task of teaching Nudge the fine manners of a housegoat I go. I decided that this would be best done when the husband is not home. Nudge accepted the condition that if he was to be in the house, it had to be on a leash. In fact, he accepted the whole process with amazing good nature. I suppose it beat living in a barn!

I soon learned that Nudge had not lost his need to be with me at all times. Nor had he forgotten our limited but clearly understood vocabulary of "Maatt!" and "mmaaa". In the summer months that he had been in the barn, he had grown considerably, a fact revealed to him when he attempted to fit into his chair. Bummer.

Nudge continued to distinguish himself from our previous goats with his vocabulary. He was a very talkative goat. Even when we were with him in the barn, he would "blah, blah, maaa, poof" all the while. The neighbors, the same Mrs. Dugdale, would often remark on the goat talk coming from our direction around feeding time. "We always know where Nudge is," they would comment. Good thing they liked goats.

But in the house, as if in some sanctuary, Nudge went mute. Except when he spotted some action outside. Standing on the baseboard and looking out the window interested him should the dogs bark or a car pull up. He would then utter "maah" to get my attention. Watch goat.

It was in my office that we spent the most time. Not necessarily the best place to have a goat considering the pile of papers that accumulate in an office. But I solved that by allowing Nudge the trash basket from which he would pull all sorts of goodies. Envelops with plastic windows were his favorite, followed by horse catalogs

and candy wrappers. The husband was responsible for the latter.

No longer able to fit under the desk as he had as a goatling, Nudge settled for under the table. With the leash hooked over my wrist I could work at the computer for hours while

Nudge napped or nibbled. There was the occasional disruption when he leapt to his feet pulling the leash and whirling me about in my swivel chair. The husband would often find us sitting amidst a pile of paper both working feverishly on our projects.

Nudge never lost his love for sinks. And warm water. My blacksmith can attest to that, having turned to place another hot shoe in his water bucket only to find it empty beside a grinning goat. Nudge would join me for a kitchen break and stand with his front legs in the sink, sipping away.

When Nudge was not in the house, he was often lounging in the enclosed porch. With winter, he quickly discovered its comforts. He had learned to work the dog doors, much to the worry of poor Kentucky Ugly who was very guarding of her dog food. The dog doors led from the porch to the garage, home of the dog food, and out. More than one delivery person thought we had three dogs until they looked closer. Most were good-natured when Nudge climbed into their truck. UPS trucks are very accessible to goats. Lesson learned, they later arrived prepared with two dog biscuits and an apple, Nudge's treat of choice.

Periodically, Nudge would want to join at us in the house. Why didn't we let him in? "Blah!", he would mutter. "Maaaah, blah, maaat, blah, poof". If we didn't respond, he would stand on his hind legs, testing the strength of the glass with his hoofs. The husband would cringe, fearing that someday a goat would crash through the door and take over his house. But that door was stronger than one would think. At twilight, such a sight could easily be construed as a small bear. Guests needed to be forewarned.

Whenever I wanted Nudge to join me, I needed only to step out on the porch and scream at the top of my lungs, "MMMMAAAHH-HH!". It would be answered with "Maahh?". Yes, "MMMMAAAH-HHH!". Since my goatspeak was street learned, I am never too sure of just what I am saying, however I am certain that the inflection on the word means something to a goat. Just like in Spanish, the inflection on the same word can mean either "T-shirt" or "prostitute" and one had best get it right when shopping in Mexico. Nudge always responded with a question to anything I said, as if to ask, "did you really mean that?" I appreciated his patience with me.

After several ""MMMMAAAHHHH!", "maahh?"s, I would see the black form running up the hill to join me. I had become somewhat unaware of how this intercourse was viewed by strangers. "Your wife speaks goat?" they would say and the husband would reply "yes, but only at the conversational level". How sweet is that?

Eventually, my goat speak was good enough to ditch the leash. The husbands desk remained a magnet for Nudge, but a sharp "MAATT!" redirected his intent and he contented himself with the trash can. Very often Nudge would follow me from the barn up to the house and join me for lunch, refusing most offerings from the table with the exception of potato chips. They were the best. He demonstrated the best of manners the entire time.

Not always so outside. He was, after all, a goat and displays of goat play to visitors was met with apprehension. Goat play is comprised of mock attacks to see if you are game, or dumb, enough to counter back. Don't do it. Unless you are me. As Nudge would rear on his hind legs, I would dive in and butt his head with my hand. Don't ever do that. But to Nudge, I was his equal and he respected my goat play by never pushing it too far. Back and forth we would go, diving and ducking, squaring off for a butt and then racing in a circle for the return.

Again, I learned from him. When the play was done, we would both bow our heads and lean on each other, not pushing, just balancing. It meant it was a good game and we're still friends. Don't try that with a goat either. Unless, after reading this, you go out and get your own goat.

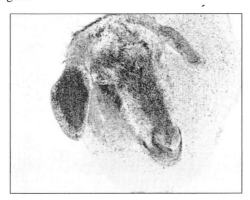

Mmmaaaahh!

My Best Dog - One

Everyone needs unconditional love; every one needs a dog.

My first experience with the "Lassie Come Home" ideology was not with a collie, but with a miniature dachshund. It was a stretch, but the concept was the same. Her name was Zimmy, and her life was wonderful.

For a dog who knew nothing of a farm, she learned very quickly that horses and goats were to be avoided at all costs, especially when you're only eight inches off of the ground. Her size had nothing to do with dogginess, the manta of dachshunds being that "size is a state of mind". Known as "her royal shortness", for fourteen years she ruled with compassion, understanding and swift justice over every one, including me.

The one advantage of being small was the ease in which one traveled in a car. Or truck. With a horse trailer attached. For an entire weekend. Camping! Camping meant food. Easy food. If there wasn't food at one's own camp, there was a camp nearby with some sucker for a cute dog who could sit up like a groundhog endlessly until thrown a little treat. We came to term this as "working the crowd" as we watched that cute little brown tail wagging in anticipation as she approached yet another unsuspecting innocent with a hot dog in their hand.

Zimmy's gastronomic feats never failed to impress me. She was so persistent at begging at a hot dog booth that someone bent down and placed a strip of mustard down her back. She once swallowed a full size hoagie while I mailed a letter at the post office. I was so amazed that a fourteen-inch dog could eat a sixteen-inch hoagie that I rushed her to the vet. He could only suggest that I not feed her again for three days and that in the future, mail my letters before hitting the deli. Two days later she was hungry again.

A trail ride pig roast was perhaps Zimmy's finest hour. I was especially busy with my horse and Zimmy was especially busy watching the pig going round and around over the fire. Wow. A roasting pig was a dachshund's dream come true, as so with twenty other larger dogs who also had also devoted their day to watching the pig.

At dinner, the nice fellow carving the meat was obviously a dog lover as he made a point to toss little pieces of pig to the pack of begging dogs as he worked. Zimmy's size had nothing to do with her ability to shoulder in with dogs three times larger than she. "I am a big dog trapped in a little dogs body" was for sure her retort if any dog questioned her presence.

Returning from dinner I discovered the area around my trailer covered with dogs, in the midst of which was my darling little dachshund with the pig leg clenched in her teeth. The bone was easily twice her size, making it impossible to carry. She had to drag it backwards with determined little jerks while at the same time keep the marauding pack from stealing it from her. Three jerks to every growl and snarl was her pace all the way from the pig spit to the sanctity of trailer. Twenty dogs, all much larger than she, truly believed that she would rip their throats out if they got one whisker closer.

The next morning, while driving home, was when I discovered that the only food that disagreed with her normally iron cast stomach was pig.

Her least favorite activity was having her nails clipped. I would force myself to do this dastardly deed, withstanding the screams of terror, the rolling of the eyes and the distressed panting, and all I had done was get out the clippers! The actual clipping was nowhere as bad as the anticipation. Zimmy was so clever as to know where I kept the clippers, and should I approach that drawer, she made for parts unknown.

We were still newlyweds when the opportunity presented itself to initiate the husband to the horrors of nail clipping the dog. I confess that I did not tell him about the anticipated reaction of the dachshund, which he still thought of as a cute, cuddly creature, for fear of scaring him off.

In my sweetest voice I turned to him and said, "Would you like to C-L-I- P the dogs N-A-I-L-S with me dear"?

Since he was madly in love with me at that time and would deny me nothing, he replied, "Of course, sweetheart", (which may very well be the last time he called me that). But why are you spelling in front of the dog, surely she can't understand when you say CLIP-PERS?"

At the word CLIPPER the growingly suspicious dog became a low flying missile to the sanctity of under the bed. Between the two of us, we could not drag her out. From that time on, we resorted to spelling the word "C-L-I-P-P-E-R" in a very soft voice, sometimes even resorting to passing notes. And the husband was wise to any task asked of him that ended with "dear".

Zimmy's small size was very helpful when it came to smuggling her into some of the best hotels in the country. However, we were not sure we were going to pull this off when we found ourselves on the fifth floor of a lovely old hotel in Northhampton, Mass. The hotel was the horse show headquarters of an event we were both officiating at. To our horror, there stood a big sign "NO DOGS" glaring at everyone who passed through the lobby. We did not want to embarrass the show and ourselves by being "kicked out" should they discover the dog, but the unusually hot weather would have made it impossible for her to stay in the car. We were trapped

Zimmy was in her geriatric years, which meant some extra potty trips during the night. Once smuggled in, this presented a problem. We surveyed our options. The fire escape at the end of the hall offered what seemed to be the answer, as the path through the halls, down the elevator and through the lobby offered too many opportunities to be caught. Pleased with such a quick solution we took Zimmy to dinner and retired.

The expected middle of the night wake up bark took the husband and Zimmy on their first trip down the fire escape. Since the fire escape door would close and lock behind him, the husband cleverly stuck a magazine in the door for his return. I only half awakened when he went out so I wasn't quite sure how long he'd been gone when I awoke again, but I knew it had been too long. I quickly dressed and rushed to the fire escape door, but when I tried to open it, it wouldn't budge. I could hear the husband on the other side, but between the air conditioners and the steel door, we couldn't make out each other's words. However, I was pretty sure he wasn't calling me "sweetheart".

As I examined the door, I suddenly realized what had happened. A late guest must have seen the door slightly ajar and pushed it shut, jamming the magazine so tightly in the door that it kept it from reopening. The only thing to do was to methodically rip the magazine up until the door loosened while the husband, in just his bathrobe, crouched on the fire escape five stories above the parking lot. It didn't take as long as the husband said it did and it was funnier than he thought it was and I did offer to take the dog out from then on.

The last night of the show we were late getting back to the hotel. The show was throwing a party in the lobby for all officials and we were obliged to attend. Since Zimmy had been smuggled back to the room earlier that evening, a potty run was absolutely necessary before we could get caught up in a party. To my surprise the husband volunteered.

I should have known that he had no intention of trying the fire escape again. Wrapping Zimmy up in his dinner jacket he confidently entered the elevator, joining two other men whom coincidentally also had dinner jackets across their arms. As they silently rode the elevator, a tail appeared and was quickly pushed back under the dinner jacket of the man to the left. This apparently affected the dinner jacket held by the man on the right as it started to bark. My husband proudly reported to me that Zimmy peered from under her jacket but never blew her cover.

Having regained their composure by the time they reached the lobby, three men, each with a jacket over their arm and a silly grin on their face, strode nonchalantly through the waiting guests, past the big "NO DOGS" sign and out the door. It was much more fun than the fire escape.

Zimmy, my first dog, and for me, the best dog.

My Best Dog - Two

At age two, Piper was still one-hundred per cent puppy. The things she did were no longer cute, so when her owners heard of the sucker who took in goats, geese and chickens, they had found their mark. Golden Retrievers are the world's happiest dogs, bouncy, full of life and adventure. They also spend a lot of time in mud puddles and are very wet, very much of the time. I thought that since I had a farm, she should fit right in.

A seventy pound bouncing, wet dog is hazardous even if they are kept outside. Piper never presented herself with an empty mouth, it was filled with road apples (horse manure, yuck!), rotten apples, rocks, and flattened dead animals from the road out front. If she had time, she would roll on the dead animal before scraping it loose from the tarmac. I started to see why she had needed to find a new home.

The move to Pennsylvania saved her. Piper grew up, overnight. Gone was the puppy and there was the grandest red dog on the best behavior you could imagine. Needless to say, this made me happy. The "new" Piper no longer pounced on every creature she could find; rather she took it as her role to protect all the farm animals in their new home. She promptly thrashed the neighbor's Weimaraner when he came for a social call because he looked the wrong way at one of the ducks. When one of the horses got loose, Piper was frantic until I caught him and returned him to his proper place. Order, which is what Piper wanted in her new home, and woe to anyone who disrupted it. I could hardly believe that this was the same dog. But I had no complaints.

Piper was the first of my dogs to accompany me and my horse on my rides. It was a realization of a childhood dream, my horse, my dog and me. I loved it. We loved it. Sometimes I would ride out for hours, Piper following me every mile with ease. But Golden Retrievers being what they are, she could hardly pass up the opportunity to carry something in her mouth.

Shortly after deer hunting season, she found the prize of all prizes. The remains of the hind leg of a deer. The entire hind leg of a deer. She just had to have it, despite its size, so grasping it in her powerful jaws she bounced back onto the trail with the free end of the leg jerking along wildly with her every stride.

My horse had a heart attack right on the spot. When I finally regained the control, I had left Piper about a mile down the trail. My horse would have been happy to leave her there forever, but I didn't want her travelling home alone. We found her sitting between two trees, bone in teeth, on a narrow section of trail. Every time she walked forward, the leg would hit the trees and Piper would back up. No way she was about to put her newly gained prize down, not for a minute.

While my horse watched disapprovingly out of the corner of her eye, I dismounted and helped Piper past the trees. Undaunted, she trotted happily along home in front of me. She was in front of me because my horse was not having anything to do with her behind me. The jointed end was doing a peculiar dance to and fro with each of Pipers stride.

My neighbor was putting his garbage out as I passed along. "Nice day, eh." He was not one for great conversation.

"Lovely," I replied, hoping he had not noticed the dog. Or the leg.

"Nice dog there, eh".

"Oh, eh, yes, she is."

"Nice bone she's got there, too."

"Oh, eh, yes, everything about us is very nice," I said, urging my horse along a bit faster. I couldn't wait to find out what my neighbors were going to say about me now. I felt I was becoming entertaining enough as it was.

The bone spent several weeks being the center of Piper's universe. She was very reluctant to leave it at home, unguarded, so she would take it along with her on our rides. There we were, woman on horse, dog with bone, trotting all about the area like this was normal. The horse did not at all appreciate any of this.

Bad as that was, it was worse at home. Piper liked to greet people with it in her mouth. The flopping leg brought all kinds of remarks. "What a pretty dog, don't you feed her?" "Did something die on the farm?" "You don't let her in the house with that, do you?"

Finally, time took its toll and it became two separate leg bones, then bone parts, and then history. But for three more years my neighbors would ask about the dog's bone.

Piper was not only a Retriever, she was also a Remover. She started with shoes. My neighbor's three school age girls had a smorgasbord of shoes on their porch for her to choose from. Piper would take one away. This caused considerable stress on the girl whose shoe was missing just as she left for school. I got an early phone call, there would be a mad search around my barn and yard and finally the tearful young lady would have her shoe. Never was there a mark on it, Piper had the true gentle mouth of a Retriever!

While Piper liked shoes the best, she would not hesitate at the opportunity to retrieve hammers, work gloves, pipe wrenches, saws, curry combs, brushes and hats. If she had simply brought these home, we could have dealt with it, but she added the twist of "rearranging" things. Neighbor A would have neighbor B's hammer, neighbor B would have neighbor C's glove and I would have a boot that no one claimed. Neighbor B would put his hat down to kiss his six-year-old and it would end up two miles down the road at neighbor D's. Piper had a territory.

Every spring when the snow melted, my lawn looked like an archeological dig. I would load up all the goodies and tote them throughout the neighborhood in an effort to find their rightful owner. It got me to know my neighbors, and their various possessions, well. At the very least, I knew who to borrow something from.

Piper was guilty of numerous unspeakable offenses against cats as a young dog. She must have felt she needed to do penance for this as she, to my surprise, happily adopted an abandoned litter of five tiny kittens. The five kittens were red, just like her, and she determinedly nursed them into healthy young cats. Other than the fact that they thought themselves Golden Retrievers, they grew up to be fairly normal.

As Piper matured, she became the best of companions. In the summer, she would share my dips in the pond with me, gliding along like the loch ness monster as we swam along together. In the winter, she bounced around my cross-country skis, constantly urging me to go faster, farther.

The day she was hit by a car was numbing. Even after three weeks of the best care at the vet hospital, her prognosis was not good. I decided to bring her home, crippled or not, she would at least be within her normal surroundings. It had been the longest separation of our lives and she had suffered in that.

Home proved the best medicine for her. The hospital personnel had been unable to get her to use her "doggie cart", an ingenious device that allowed her to be mobile in her front while wheeling her back legs along. . She was ecstatic about being home again. The depressed attitude vanished, and the happy dog came back.

Completely forgetting about the cart behind her, she resumed her role as the neighborhood retriever as if everything was normal. It was a bit unnerving to sight a sixty pound red dog on wheels tooling down the road, but people were getting used to expecting odd things from us. Seems that my neighbors actually missed being visited by my dog, even the little girls whose shoes were still a top priority to Piper.

Piper's rehabilitation was slow but progressive. When not in her cart, she was confined to a kiddy pool in my kitchen filled with horse bedding for her comfort. She could squirm around, but that was about it. She tried as hard as I prayed for to regain control of her hind legs. On the eve of Christmas, my dog got up and walked for the first time in four months. It was the best Christmas present I ever had.

It was the eve of Christmas, seven years later, that I had to part with my lovely red dog. The injury was causing her to suffer, and I had made her a promise. She spent the morning at her favorite spot, overlooking the barn basking in the sunlight. She had had a long and wonderful life, and we smiled to each other as she bid me good-bye. I knew I could never replace her. Piper was the best dog.

My Best Dog - Three

My finest moments in life were spent with my German Shepherd, "Waab". I still drove an old Omni, left over from my school teaching salary days, which served ever so well as a farm car. I never drove it alone; it was always filled with dogs, first Waab, then Saab, son of Waab. I would open the door and they would leap into the backseat whining with the anticipation of the short, but obviously joyous, trip to the barn.

The car was safe from theft. Partially because if you saw two huge German Shepards panting out the window, you would consider another car. Even if the Shepards were not in it, you would consider another car. The car smelled of dog two parking places away. We figured we could leave the keys in it, running, and it would still be there when we came back.

It was at the barn where a dog found heaven. Goats to chase, horses to herd, boarders with children, children with food. It was a grand place for a dog. Waab loved every body. But Waab saved a special part of the barn experience just for me.

Whenever I saddled my favorite, and fastest, horse, Waabb would "woo-woo" for joy. No one else joined us for this ritual; it was "our" thing. Just the three of us, and the possibility of racing the hill. Not too steep, not too long, but perfect for a carefree gallop in hand. I'm not sure which one of us liked that hill the most, the horse, the dog or me.

Of course, I didn't always race the hill; there were many times I didn't include it in my ride for one reason or another. But on the days I felt I needed a lift, my horse and my dog knew the moment I turned onto that trail, "we're going to race, we're going to top the hill"!

Waabb always started even with me, right below my right stirrup. It was his concession in making it a fair race. As soon as I signaled the horse to go, we three were off like a shot. As my horse sprang into the first stride, Waab was left behind. By the second stride he was gaining, and by the third stride he was again exactly at my right stirrup, matching stride for stride the effort of my horse. If I had bent down over the horse's neck, I could have easily petted him in the head.

Like clockwork, two thirds of the way up the hill Waabb would raise his head with a big doggy grin, look me straight in the eye and say, "can't you get that thing to go any faster?" and, ""poof"", he was gone. He just loved beating my horse up that hill.

Being a German Shepherd, he took his role as protector very seriously. Anyone was welcome at the farm, or even in our yard. But put one foot into the house and a soft, yet firm set of jaws clamped around one's ankle. Perhaps it was Waab's subtle approach to being a watchdog that made him so effective. No one ever questioned his authority.

Waab was to me what Rin Tin Tin was to Rusty. Loyal. Protecting. Affectionate. Handsome. Caring. Devoted. If he were a person, I would have married him on the spot. He did not have to do anything special to be special. And not only was he special, he made me feel special.

When I finally laid him to rest I could not imagine having another dog, and did not attempt to look for one. Waab was the best dog.

My Best Dog - Four

If I ever felt "manipulated" by fate, it was so in finding Ugly. I didn't know I was going to Kentucky until the day we left. It was an impulsive trip, and not one that I was entirely sure of. We left with two trucks, five horses, three dogs and a cat. We encountered all kinds of problems getting there, including getting the trailer stuck on a rock for four hours in a pasture where we bivouacked for the night.

But there to greet me when we finally pulled into the campgrounds in Kentucky was Ugly. She acted like she was expecting us. All week she stayed under our trailer, shyly accepting food but not letting us any closer. We all figured her to be the camp dog who worked the crowd on a regular basis. Even with the arrival of over a hundred more trailers, she never left us. She had made her choice.

I couldn't help but inquire at the camp office about her. The nice man at the office knew immediately when he saw a sucker and played me like a fine tuned instrument.

"Yep, that there dawg you are talking about we named "Ugly", sad little thang. Showed up here in the spring and has been working that end of camp all summer. Don't know what'll become of her when winter sets in…no one here but the boys who check on the place once or twice a week. 'Suppose we should call in the game warden…he takes care of stray dawgs…if you know what I'm sayn'? Unless ya'll would want to take her home with ya?"

What could I say?

My new dog, the wet, smelly, flea-infested and probably pregnant dog, greeted me with newfound affection. I had to admit she was really pretty darn ugly. She was cross eyed, spindly and looked more than a little bit feral. Despite the prospect of a new home, any efforts to catch her were fruitless. Finally I just opened up the trailer door and she jumped in. She made it clear that she would have nothing to do with a collar or rope, but should I wish to pick her up and carry her, that was fine. I could sense the fear in her body, but her eyes were trustful. She had known a kind master before; it would just take time for her to trust again.

On the way home we decided to name her "Kentucky Ugly", a forever reminder of where she had come from. The poor husband was still in shock that I had adopted such a pathetic creature, but he figured it was my decision and my problem.

I was right, she was pregnant. And she had every parasite known to dogs. How she tolerated a bath and a visit to the vet in the first week we had her is to her credit as a darn nice dog. She was still terrified of quick movements and refused to even eat in my presence. It took three months to convince her to come into the house and six months before visitors could pet her. Whatever events had led her my way, they were not all happy ones. I shudder to think what would have become of her had I not made that unplanned trip to Kentucky.

She is now my constant companion; her herding instincts necessitating that I not disappear from her sight. Like Piper and Waab before her, going for a ride with me is her favorite event of the day. We sing this silly song together;

> *Happy Dog I am*
> *See me wag my tail*
> *Happy Dog I am*
> *When I'm on the trail*

The husband balked at continuing to call her "Ugly". Even my neighbor got on my case and started calling her "Beautiful". "Here, Beautiful, here girl". I took her along with me on a nice pleasure ride with some friends from Virginia. Maggy noticed the dog and said, "what did you call her? Ugly?". I said yes. "Good name for her." For the fact remained, she was still one ugly dog.

Just what is in a name? So what, her name was "Ugly". As an adjective, ugly means "lacking appealing physical features, especially facial ones". Yep, got that right. But I was using "Ugly" as a noun, as a name, which actually worked for this dog. She was downright scary. Seen at a distance she would surely be mistaken for a coyote. Without her collar, surely she would have been shot. I am sure she never attached any detrimental meaning to her name, she was simply, "Ugly".

I never trained her. Her ability to understand my cues was a tribute to her intelligence. A friend came one day and offered a treat if she would sit. She did. And did so ever since. She could be running up the driveway and I could yell "sit!", and she would. The husband doesn't even come close to being that responsive!

In the winter just the sight of me taking down my snow shoes sent her spinning in circles of joy. Her shiny coat and happy face no longer told the story of a starved, mistreated dog. Visitors marveled at her obedience and uncanny understanding of how to be a perfect dog. This was all her decision and she fitted in perfectly with our lives.

Even now, when I feel her nudge my hand, whether I am at the computer or stretched out on the couch, I remain in awe that such a dog let me into her life. She had no reason to believe in me. But she did.

I can't help but feel that Waab sent her, for no one should be without a dog. And now, she is the best dog!

You Are Never Too Old
To Outgrow Your Pony

Her mother was so impressive that the moment Steve saw her he just knew he had to have her. He drove all the way from Vermont to Florida and back when he finally talked his way into buying her. Pleased as punch, he arrived home only to find that everyone else that saw her just knew that they had to have her. Some horses have charisma, this mare had that, plus attitude.

Louise was one of those people who had to have her. She finally wrangled a deal with Steve to get the mare in foal and brought her to a prize Morgan stallion. She bred her all spring and all summer. Nothing. In bitter disappointment, the mare returned to Vermont and was turned out with the farms Arabian stallion. As Louise puts it, eleven months and ten minutes later, "Cavalletti" was born.

Louise wasted no time driving to Vermont to claim her baby. Surely this was the offspring of her prize Morgan stallion. No, said Steve, it was the Arab sire. Money was offered, tears were shed, but Louise went home empty handed.

Ten years later I was visiting Steve at his winter farm in Georgia when he pulled out a hairy little black mare for me to ride. "Isn't she just the cutest", he said. Somewhere under the bushy black mane the mare was sizing me up and I got the distinct sensation that I was about to learn about my limitations.

Steve swung up on his big champion endurance horse (which was, by the way, her half brother) and I stepped into the saddle on the camparitively diminitive Cavalletti. Leaving no opportunity for introductions, Steve took off. The smile I was wearing had something to do with gritting my teeth. While Steve's mount cruised down the trail, mine hopped and skittered all over the place. Oblivious of my fate, Steve was having the best time of it and I knew better than to complain. After all, I was an endurance rider!

After about ten miles, we came to a walk and Steve looked back to see how things were going…well…I was still on, wasn't I? "How did she go? Did you like her? She's really something isn't she? I think she could really compete. Why don't you ride her at the next competition?", he blathered at me.

"Well, to tell the truth, " I was trying to be polite, "she's a bit green, don't you think?"

Laughing, he said, "well yeah, you're the first person to ride her!"

I knew it!

Cavalletti continued her training process on the trail. I rode her 100 miles in NJ and was Reserve Champion. I rode her 100 miles in New York and was Champion. I rode her in Vermont and came in second. By the end of the season we declared her broke and she was declared the East Coast One Hundred Mile Champion. By golly, Steve was right!

Just like her mother before her, Cavalletti had an aura that made everyone who saw her want to take her home. The next year at the Florida One Hundred Mile Ride, Steve announced that she was for sale. Good grief, people marched up to him with checkbook in hand and told him to name his price! People intercepted me on the trail, in the barn, while walking to the porta potty asking what it would take for Steve to part with her. I was the wrong person to ask, I was quite fond of the little black mare and hated seeing her go. Steve's wife was so upset about it that she had stopped talking to him. But Steve was enjoying the show.

We were out grazing the horses when Louise walked up to us. She had never faltered from her belief that Cavalletti was hers in the first place. Bravely she approached Steve with her checkbook and announced that she was going to take her horse home this time. But when Steve told her the price, I saw Louise's face crumple and fighting back her tears, had to close her inadequate checkbook and walk away empty handed, again.

"That was mean", I blurted out to Steve, who really wasn't a "mean" person at all.

"Don't you think she is worth that price", he returned with a challenge.

"Yes, I mean no, I mean, she is priceless. Money shouldn't decide," I turned and met Steve right in the eye., "she should go where she will be appreciated the most. "

We rode in silence the next day. I tried not to think that this would be my last ride on Cavalletti. Like the star she was, Cavalletti won the ride, a bittersweet ending for me. I flew home the next day not knowing where she went.

When I pulled into my driveway in Vermont, there sat Steve.

What? He offered to take me to lunch and in my confused "how the heck did you get here before I did" state, I agreed.

I was still upset about Cavalletti so I avoided mentioning anything about her. Until he brought it up. Bracing myself, he started to tell me about all the people that wanted to buy her. Yadda, yadda, yadda, I was so squirming by the time he told me that he had made a decision. But first, could I do him a favor. Oh, geesh, sure, it was a big favor, whatever, just tell me where the mare is!

"She's on a trailer headed to Vermont."

"What?"

"You told me that I could not let her go to anyone that could not appreciate her, right?"

"Right"

"Well, I looked around and realized that no one could appreciate her more than you, it was so simple"

"She's mine?", I gulped.

"For the favor. You were right, like her mother, no price could be put on that mare"

I cried.

Cavalletti came home and took over the farm. Just seeing her in my pasture brought a smile to my face. She continued to win every ride and was once again named East Coast One Hundred Mile Champion.

There are a few little things about Cavalletti that need mentioning. Like her attitude. There is nothing like riding a mare with attitude, but sometimes there was a tad too much for comfort. Having been trained "on the fly", literally, Cavalletti had missed some of the finishing points that most horses acquire during training. Come to think of it, she probably would have ignored them anyway.

Riding Cavalletti was like putting notes into a suggestion box. I would come up with an idea, submit it, wait for her to review it and she would eventually get back to me. Quite often her answer had nothing to do with my suggestion. She often pointed out to me that I was just sitting up on her back while she was down there doing all of the work. I should remember my place. Her manta was, "don't be riding me, I know what I'm doing!" And she did!

In her determination to keep me humble, Cavalletti dumped me periodically. Getting dumped off of a 13.2 hand pony in public is embarrassing, very embarrassing, and a high point of entertainment for my fellow riders! One time she got so mad at me she stood straight up in a streambed into which I landed with both feet. Another time she was cruising along an open trail and dropped her shoulder so fast that I bit into the sand with my face. That was a good one, because the gal I was riding with stopped, horrified, and stated, "I thought you were a good rider!"

Cavalletti was tough!

The day she came up lame still brings me to tears. Who knows what happened but the x-rays were severe enough to end her career. Rest, like several years worth, would heal it, but there would always be an issue. Grateful I was to have had the opportunity to careen through the woods on this little marvel, but I wanted more. Babies! She could have babies!

The reason I had ended up with Cavalletti in the first place was because Steve had believed that no one should have her that could not appreciate her. The only person that I knew of that could appreciate her more than I was Louise. So, I called her. Although we did not know each other well, we were fellow trail riders and shared a deep love for a little black mare with an attitude. Louise finally realized her dream by taking Cavalletti home and breeding her to her prize Morgan stallion. Cavalletti will live on in her fine black son. Just like his mother, and his grandmother before her, everyone who sees him just knows that they had to have him. But after waiting fifteen years, Louise is not about to give up her pony.

Down the Drain

The moment I walked into my bedroom I knew some-thing was missing. What was now an unconscious act for me was a result of a lifetime of association with creatures who used every sense plus that sixth one. I could pick up that there was something wrong with a horse before my eyes could find it. I knew how many times Oaf waddled across the bed for a mid-night snack without ever waking up. I could make a mental note to be careful where I stepped in the morning after hearing a cat woof up dead bird parts in the wee hours while I slept. The lack of ferret-presence feel-ing therefore hit me right in the face

Confronted with the problem of my missing ferret I referred to past experience. Somewhere in my brain I kept notes of what-to-do-if scenarios. The notes were kept by a little wizard. Kind of like the office assistant in a computer that pops up when you need help then walks you through things like writing a letter. "It looks like you are writing a letter, can I help?" My computer office assistant was a cat who did cute things like lick its paws and purr while sleeping. I have never seen my brain wizard, but judging by personality, it's probably a female cat.

"Did you leave the bedroom door open?" – No. "Then she must be in the room, just hiding." OK. Out came the checklist. "Under bed covers- no. In the top shelf of the sweater closet – no. Under the husbands dinner jackets (he need not know) – no. In the ferret box – no. In the toy box?- NO. Well, you must have left the door open!"

While I was dealing with feelings of guilt that I had, indeed, left the door open for a teeny weeny second when I dashed in to grab a sweater earlier that day, the brain wizard was scouring for the where-to–look-when-the-ferret-escapes-into-the-house checklist. A brain wizard is very helpful in such cases as one has a tendency to panic. Out came the list. Remove all dogs and cats from the area of the search. This was underlined because of past omission of this rule which resulted in hours of searching for a ferret tucked into a corner hiding from curious canine and feline noses. Lockdown of the cats and dogs returned me to the list. Look in the spare bedroom – no. Open the shower door – no. Rummage through the spare clothes the husband likes to keep behind the door – no. Check the plants in the living room (right, ferrets love to dig in plants) – darn, plants look fine.

The wizard was getting a tad annoyed. No ferret meant going to the upstairs list and that list was a long one. There were a lot of places for a ferret to hide up there, this could take days! But as soon as I started the charge up the stairs I was blocked by a closed door. Hey, the door is closed, I remarked. I can see that said the wizard, who was now rummaging about for the look-in-the-cellar checklist which was even longer and more time consuming. I hope you have nothing better to do, the wizard hissed, driving home the guilt of having left the bedroom door open for that teeny weeny moment. If I did have something to do, it was going to have to wait until I found my ferret.

Ferret, verb, meaning "to search in an area persistently". Synonyms; Search. Hunt. Rummage. Furrow. Dig out. Flush. Force out. That was what I was thinking of as I headed for the basement. We had a big basement. Full of stuff. Plenty of places for me to search, hunt, rummage, furrow, dig out and flush. But the moment I hit the bottom step my sixth sense jerked my head to the left where I laid my eyes on the basement floor drain lid NOT covering the drain. Staring back at me was a perfect hole emptying into who knows where that no self respecting ferret could turn up. I felt panic but even worse, the wizard dropped her comforting, efficient, stay calm demeanor and screamed - THE FERRET HAS LEFT THE BUILDING!

Dropping to the floor, I peered down into the drain hole. It smelled earthy. Probably because it ended in some hole somewhere out on the lawn. Great. The pipe teed about eight inches down which only increased the options for the ferret who most likely had gleefully tunneled herself into the hole and ran with uncontained fervor toward wherever it led her. I just prayed it was not into something nasty for ferrets. The wizard was pretty hysterical, citing the odds of recovering a ferret once it found the great outdoors. After all they were wild animals and could not be blamed for wanting to be free. But I also knew the odds for survival. I was wishing that the darn wizard would shut up!

The only helpful bit if information the wizard was able to give me was that time was of the essence. I needed to come up with a plan and do it fast. Since the wizard had no experience in ferret hunting

outside of the house, I was pretty much on my own. Think like a ferret I told myself.

First thing was to go back to step one - Remove all dogs and cats from the area of the search. Since I could not be one hundred per cent sure that the ferret had left the building, I decided to secure both the inside and the outside of the house. The dogs went into the kennel and the cats were locked upstairs. That done I was out of ideas.

The wizard was nagging me with some information I had read about ferrets when I had first acquired one years ago. It was one of those "Ferrets Make Excellent Pets" books that you get from the pet store when making the purchase of your new ferret. It talked about what to feed them, how often to exercise them and tips on what to do should you lose your ferret. Hmmm. Something about making a specific noise when feeding them so that they would associate the noise with food and come to you. The book suggested a bell or whistle, sound advice that I had chosen to ignore. The only noise I had ever made to my ferret was endearing little kisses. Kiss, kiss. Kiss kiss. And she would lick me back. All this did was make me miss my ferret even more.

I was getting depressed. I returned to the bedroom hoping that I had missed something and that a cute little masked face would pop out from the husbands shirts and I would laugh at this new place to hide. I tried on the feeling of having the closet and bathroom to myself and didn't like it one bit. I would miss having to keep my watches in a drawer so they would not be stolen. I would miss brushing my teeth with a ferret twirling in the sink. Showers would be lonely and I wouldn't need to wear socks to bed to keep my feet from being attacked under the covers. I felt lonely, very, very lonely.

Thanks to the wizard screaming in my brain I took to searching for the ferret again with renewed vigor. Cat food. She only eats cat food. OK, she nibbles on the soap bar from time to time, but cat food is her favorite. Pulling down the Have A Heart trap from the upper shelf of the garage, I looked around for a good place to set it. Geesh, there were too many good places.

Thinking of the drain as a good place I started to look to see where it could possibly come out on the lawn. No luck. Grabbing a compass, I returned to the basement to orientate the direction of the pipe. While doing that it occurred to me that perhaps she might still be in the pipe. Ferrets were known for taking naps and what better place to take a nap than in one's own hole. Dropping to the floor, I once again put my face to the drain and again noted the earthy wisps of air coming from it. I had no doubt, no doubt at all that this pipe led outside.

The words from "Ferrets Make Excellent Pets" came back to me and I figured that if someone wrote a book about ferrets that perhaps they knew a thing or two. Since I had failed to take the advice of the bell or whistle, I reckoned that kissing noises were the next best thing. Kiss, kiss. Kiss, kiss, I chirped into the hole. Immediately I saw the error of my method. While a bell or whistle could be heard for miles, it was darn hard to kiss louder than ten feet. Banking on the acoustic attributes of pipes, however, I continued. Kiss, kiss. Kiss, kiss. Whoever thought that I would be lying on the floor of our basement kissing into a drain pipe. It was such a good thing that the husband was not here to see this!

Well, the kiss thing did not produce a ferret and eventually I felt pretty stupid so I quit. Returning to the idea of using the compass to find the drain outlet on the lawn, I scouted about but produced nothing. A fog of dispair was closing in around me. I had lost my ferret. I tried not to cry.

The darn wizard would not leave me alone so I perked back up and listened to the voice inside of me. THINK LIKE A FERRET! More importantly, think like YOUR ferret. My ferret had never ever seen the great outdoors. She had been born in a cage in Michigan, flown east, driven to the pet store then came home with me. She, like her parents and their parents, knew absolutely nothing about finding food in the wild. Therefore, after thirty hours of being "free", she would be darn hungry.

I had already dropped cat food bits all around the house, but thinking more was better I went into the garage to get myself a big ol' bucket of the stuff. While leaning down into the cat food barrel (if you have seven cats, you have a barrel, not a bag, of cat food) I felt my six sense tap me on the shoulder.

Standing on my feet, in her accustomed manner, was my ferret, looking more than put out that she had gone through such an experience. I had total meltdown, blurted out all kinds of ferret kisses and ran with her into the house as fast as I could, slamming every door behind us until we were safe in the bedroom. I then placed her on the floor and watched her happily scurry to her water bottle slurping down a gallon or two of the stuff. Apparently domestic ferrets can't figure out how to get water in the wild either.

I believe my ferret survived the experience better than I. Nor had I realized just how much I liked sharing my room with a little weasel, even if she did steal my watch from time to time.

Weighing Options

I have come to the opinion that the sport of distance riding is so demanding for women because the competition is divided up, not by ability, not by sex, but by weight. Somebody is always dropping a bath room scale in front of you commanding you to step on it with all of your tack. No woman over the age of fifty even owns a bathroom scale, let alone gets on one.

As if that is not bad enough, many competitions take diabolical pleasure in insuring that not only you, but the world, knows your weight division by the color of your number. We all get the opportunity to eye up our fellow riders and contemplate the actual weight of the saddle in relation to the color borne.

As you ride with your number announcing like a scarlet letter your weight, your friends comment, "oh, you're not in my division any more, new saddle?"

They know darn well that it's the same saddle, some friends. Not to leave any question in anyone's mind, weight division results are published monthly in a national magazine.

We should all get gold stars.

This scenario is what brings us to working out in a gym in the winter months. Those finely honed bodies of summer can deteriorate with terrifying speed after a successful holiday season. We could

tell how desperate someone was by how fast they jumped at the first suggestion of hitting the gym. Not everyone was game for the idea, but one comment about riding in the HEAVYWEIGHT division come Spring got them into action.

We overcame all kinds of obstacles. The twenty-year old bathing suit that finally failed to leave the pool with its body. Meeting someone you know while stark naked in the showers. Forgetting your underwear for the trip home. But the biggest obstacle of all was lunch.

To treat ourselves after the workout was lunch at the local country store. Before even entering the door, it was decided that a veggie sandwich and water was the regimented fare. It was here, despite our enthusiasm for the project, that we met our nemesis. Cookies. The big ones with gobs of nuts and chocolate hanging out of them. The ones the girls have set up by the register so you cannot escape their shape, color and scent when you pay your tab. Sometimes it was too much.

"We're needing incentive here girls", I stated, "I suggest a weigh in".

Problem was, no one had a scale. We were all over 50! Here is where I made my mistake; I shared this with the husband. So, what do you think he gave me for Valentine's Day?

That act has freed all men for all time the pressure of being accused of giving an inappropriate gift to their wives on such a special occasion. No matter what they give, no matter how surprised their wife might be, they can always say, "at least it's not a bathroom scale, honey", and she will have to forgive him. I am surprised that there hasn't been a statue of the husband erected in town, but maybe they are working on it in secret.

My friends communicated their thoughts about the scale with their respective husbands, emphasizing just how they would take such a gift in no uncertain terms. Not only did I now have this scale, but also it claimed that I weighed six pounds more that I thought I did. The husband's futile attempt to explain that it was all muscle was not working.

"They don't measure your muscles when they put you on that scale," I snapped, "they measure your fat!"

The husband, desperate to set all this right, came up with a brilliant idea.

"It needs to be calibrated. Just take the scale to the doctor's office and compare it with a hospital scale!"

I could just see myself with my little bag, sitting in the waiting room explaining to the nurse that I was simply there to calibrate my bathroom scale. I did it anyway, and lucky for the husband, the six pounds not only came off, but also two more came with them.

Out of guilt, the husband hired for me a personal trainer. Cool. The personal trainer introduced us to the weight room where my friend was immediately drawn to a machine.

"What's this one for?" she chirped, reaching up for the bar above her head.

As she griped, her toes flew from the floor and there she was, dangling like a frog on a hook. No need to get the scale, all we had to do was remove the ten-pound weights one by one until she dropped to the floor to know her weight.

From the rowing machine, to the treadmill, to the weight room we went. It was inevitable that being competitive types that we were bored in no time flat. Then the personal trainer mentioned racket ball. Hmmm, that didn't sound boring, but then again, we didn't have a clue what racket ball was.

Racket ball is "a fast, exciting indoor game in which the players hit a ball against the four walls of a court" according to the World Book Encyclopedia. That is, until we took over the game. The nice girl at the counter handed us two rackets, a ball and a set of rules.

"Oh, we don't need rules", we said, thanking her. "We're just going to have some fun."

The first surprise was the ball. The little bugger had a mind of it's own and obviously had much more experience than we did. Then there were the rackets. With the ball coming ever so nicely, for a change, right at us, with plenty of time to set up the swing, the racket would develop a hole just big enough to allow the ball to pass right on by.

We began to worry how long it was going to take us to make it to the Racquetball World Championships, being competitive types that we were. We asked for a less experienced ball and rackets without big holes in them. The nice girl at the desk smiled, but wisely kept her comments to herself. We finally were reduced to the point that we read the rules.

Deciding the rules were no fun, we resolved that since we were using a ball, that any game that used a ball could be incorporated into our play. Therefore, volleyball, basketball, baseball and golf applied. We could spike the ball as in volleyball, get points if we hit the window as in basketball, could take three swings at the ball before we were out as in baseball and could putt as in golf.

Despite ourselves, we got to be pretty good at racquetball. Never, never, never underestimate the backhand of a person who rides a Morgan horse. I knew the moment my partner started back riding in the early spring. The ball hit the wall, roared by my ear about ninety miles an hour, hit the back wall, roared by my other ear doing eighty and was well on it's way back before it quit.

"Oops", she said.

The only bad part about our workouts was that when we took the personal trainer to lunch; she ate the cookies.

Bad weather was a problem. If we couldn't ride and we couldn't get to the gym, we were faced with hundreds of household tasks we had put off for years. One week of ice and snow and we were reduced to cleaning out drawers. You know, outta sight, outta mind type drawers. Ones that we had not ventured into since we last moved. It became an obsession, one that netted me over eighty dollars in change that I used to support my racquetball habit.

One day my racquetball partner confessed that she had cleaned behind her refrigerator. Geesh, to have to resort to that. I went home, shaking my head for her shame, only to feel my own refrigerator calling to me. I resisted for two days, but finally pulled the sucker out and vacuumed up three ossified mouse bodies, eight pounds of cat hair and a family of spiders. We both went on a rampage of cleaning behind everything in the house for a week. Thank goodness the weather improved!

Spring would take us back to the barn but also bring the first ride weigh-in. We stepped on that scale with confidence, staring the diabolical weigh-in clerk right in the eye.

"Light weight," he would announce.

"Whew!"

The Junior Hunt

It was our junior hunt. Fox hunting, while primarily an adult sport, knows that it's future lies in the kids. So it's a big deal, members going to 4-H and pony club meetings, talking up the sport and offering advise for first timers. The large turnout was a tribute to their success at painting a picture of hounds running over hill and dale, horses in calm pursuit to the music of the hunt horn borne by our scarlet clad huntsman. We hoped not to disappoint.

Fox hunting is the root of all of those hunter shows where an outside sport is reduced to inside a ring where impeccable jumps are laid out on impeccable footing over which impeccable horses carry their young charges. Something of the wild adventure of foxhunting is lost in having the riders count every stride between each fence. The only thing a foxhunter counts on is luck.

Somewhere along the line someone noticed that perhaps the hunter sport had strayed a bit from it's roots and suggested to young riders that they should experience the real thing at least once in their life. Therefore, our invitation to "ride the field" was met with entusiastic, but nervous anticipation by our guests.

The junior hunt is also the day to thank our regular junior riders by allowing them to perform the duties of "staff". They get to "whip in", lead the field and control the hounds. With "staff" right with them just in case, of course. In other words, it was a big day.

The weather gods were certainly with us serving up a warm autumn day with a cobalt ski and perfect scenting conditions. Hounds, having to scent their quarry no higher than their noses, need a slowly warming day to keep on the line of scent. No matter how many foxes out there, once that scent is over their heads, the hounds are lost.

We started out slowly, casting the hounds in an open field so everyone could watch them work. There were a few short runs, just enough to give the kids a bit of a thrill. I was riding second field, where the more timid riders hang out. We had three girls and a parent with us, all a bit nervous but happy to be there. The second field master, the husband, and myself were in charge of keeping it that way.

Eventually the huntsman moved the hounds down the road and into a glen with a creek crossing. Considering the type of trappy country we hunted, each field carried a two-way radio for safety. Mine crackled out, "watch for the bees at the creek, " just as we approached the creek. Geesh. As calmly as we could we herded our wards through the creek and pulled up on the other side, relieved to have avoided the bees. "Correction", sputtered the radio, "the bees are on the far side of the creek." We were standing on the far side of the creek.

No need to tell us that we had, indeed, found the bees as one of the girls started screaming and her horse started stomping. He stomped so hard he backed into a tree, pitching his rider onto his neck, which he was shaking with all of his might. We stood in open-mouthed horror thinking the worst but somehow she stayed with it as the horse bolted to safety. Whew. The radio opened again, "hello, second field, did you get the message about the bees?" I didn't bother to answer.

We quietly moved our group towards the rest of the field, all the while telling our somewhat shaken junior what a great job she did. They don't have bees at hunter shows. As we entered a wooded area a fallen tree beckoned a jumping opportunity. After all, hunters jump. Three of our charges had a most pleasant hop over and were gathered on the other side feeling rather smug when the fourth horse, who up to that point had been standing quietly watching the others jump, for lack of words, tossed a hissy fit. It was a leap; all four legs left the ground about 3 feet into the air. Then a twist and a landing first on the hind legs, then the fore. Amazingly, the rider stayed on.

We were again, wide mouthed with surprise. The field master, in the manner of an accomplished horsewoman who didn't abide by horses having hissy fits, grabbed the bridle just as the horse did an encore. No warning. No reason. Just bad horse etiquette. The rider, still unbalanced by the first leap didn't have a chance. She and the horse parted company at the apex of the leap sailing her through the air in what we all swore was slow motion before she landed in a heap on the ground. Thud.

No, no, no, this was not what we had planned for the introduction to fox hunting to little girls who didn't ride outside of a ring but rarely. The girl was severely shaken, but not hurt, to our relief, but our little group was huddled together as if perhaps they were next. The bee sting girl was starting to cry. No, no, we had to save this.

The field master started delving out commands. You, take the horse, you take over the field until I am back, and you stop crying.

It was fox hunting in its truest form as we all did as told. To me fell the leading of the field, which I gathered up and exited the area as quickly as possible. We needed to catch up with the main field, get the girls back into the thrill of the hunt and put all of this behind us.

My timing could not have been worse. Considering the scenarios we had just been through none of us had been paying attention to the radios. Otherwise we would have known that the field was but a short way from us in a clearing where they were desperately regrouping the hounds after one of the juniors horses had accidently taken the tip of Envy's tail off with his hoof.

I rode right into Envy with my group, and she was so happy to see us she wagged her tail with fervor spraying a fine stream of blood over us all. Of all days to pick a white horse to ride. Realizing my faux pas, I looked to the huntsman for direction but she was busy sneaking a well-deserved snort from her flask. What a day!

The awaiting group of parents looked a bit concerned after watching a riderless horse be returned to his trailer followed by a blood-spattered group of young ladies. There isn't much blood in the hunter show world. But to their credit, they exclaimed nothing but happiness for their adventures and promised to be back next year. Ah, kids.

Boiled Owls

A few years back my good friend Irving McNaughton was sharing his philosophy of trail riding with those lunching with him. The only thing Irving loves more than horses, and he can't help himself as he is from Maine, is the telling of stories.

"Years ago I can remember going to competitions and seeing withered, weathered, worn trail riders, many past their riding years, with program in hand, sharpened pencil ready to make notes as every horse was presented to the judges. For days they lurked about the barns, they spied on horses on the trail, and they made short, concise comments after each horse trotted out.

"Looks a bit off to me, judge must be blind",

"Wouldn't want that in my barn",

"Not worth feeding",

"Who is this judge, anyway?"

"My grandmother wouldn't be able to miss that!"

"They were all tough, rough trail riders who had ridden every ride imaginable in every type of weather imaginable and could tell you about the time they fell off a cliff and still finished the ride. They could rattle off the breeding of every horse they had ever ridden and every horse that they had ever ridden with. They knew more about shoeing, vetting, feeding, saddle making, bits and riding attire than any one alive. They rode before electrolytes, heart monitors, riding tights, sports bras, easy boots and orthopedic stirrups. They could show you their scars made by decades of riding in blue jeans. They were the toughest things to be found in the woods and.....if they were found in the Maine woods, they would be called "boiled owls"".

Irving made it clear that in his mind there was special group of riders automatically "grandfathered" as "boiled owls" and rattled off their names. Others, such as we, were in his eyes, "owls in the making".

The next time we heard about "boiled owls" was again in Maine. A nice guy named Denny Emerson joined us. Denny was an Olympic Gold Medallist in Combined Training, but a rookie to endruance riding. He was polling the riders as to their various takes on the sport. Irving went into his "boiled owl" story and got a good laugh. What Irving didn't know is that Denny writes for a national publication, "The Chronicle of the Horse", nor did he know that Denny had experienced the covey of "boiled owls" that lurked around trail rides. He knew exactly what Irving was talking about!

Seems that Denny got to thinking that combined training could use a few more "boiled owls' rather than "princesses" and made this point in his next article. Then Denny gets quoted in another magazine. Irving is sitting watching ESPN on television and the coach for the New Zealand team sums up his riders by calling them "boiled owls". Irving fell out of his chair. The entire world knew about "boiled owls"!

Irving is now famous. Of course, it went to his head. We go to rides and he is busy telling whomever of us to "buck up" when the going got tough so that we can attain "boiled owl" status. No quitting just because it is pouring buckets of rain, no complaining about the heat, no pulling just because your horse lost three shoes, no asking someone to trot your horse out just because you just got kicked in the shin, no excuse to not ride because your a)girth doesn't fit, b)broke your bridle, c)forgot all of your riding clothes or d)your horse is lame,;

BORROW IT AND FINSH!

We became known as the "boiled owls in training". No one was sure if this was a good thing or a bad thing, but we all loved Irving and went along with it.

Irving's a boiled owl himself, although he doesn't think so. He's a tall barrelchested man with long knobby legs that bow out with every step he takes. He refuses to tell his age, but he is no kid. He has to ride a big horse, not easy when dealing with Arabs who are little spindly creatures. Yet Irving has a magnificent big horse, competing in one hundred-mile rides throughout the Northeast.

We were in Puxatawny, Pennsylvania, riding a hundred mile ride in the pouring rain. It had rained all day, making the trail treacherous in places. One particular hill was simply a trough of slippery clay. As we slid down it, we spotted Irving ahead. His horse was carefully negotiating the trail but Irving was nervous.

"Don't pass", he warned.

Passing was hardly an option, the trail rutted at least two feet into the hillside.

Suddenly, Irving disappeared over his horse's head. All but his legs. His legs, encased in Ronald Mc Donald-like red and white-stripped stockings, were sticking straight up on either side of his horse's neck. His head was underwater in the stream below. His horse, thank goodness, stood perfectly still.

We could hear bubbles coming from the water.

Helpless, the best we could offer was to yell, "Kick, Irving, kick your legs free from the stirrups!"

The red and while stockings went into action, flailing wildly until finally free.

Plop, went Irving.

"Irving, are you OK?" I shouted.

"I'm not sure," he blubbered.

Landing on his head as he did worried us. Having his upside down head under water worried us more. What if he had a concussion? What if he couldn't get back on his horse? What if we had to stop to take care of him and lose precious time? Hey, this was a race.

"Do you know where you are?" we queried.

"Yep, I'm lying in a streambed in Puxatawny, Pennsylvania."

"Good, do you know why you are here?"

'Yep, because I am not a good enough rider to make it down that blasted hill."

He was fine. So we put him back on his horse and he finished the ride uneventfully.

As the self-ordained "boiled owl" maker, Irving rose to a status previously unknown to us. Irving would appear out of the mist and proclaim a rider a "boiled owl" after witnessing some act of horsemanship that most sane people would never consider. Such as; riding a hundred miles throwing up with the stomach flu; nursing a newborn baby at each vet stop for fifty miles; refusing medical attention until after finishing the ride; timing chemotherapy between riding events. Things like that got Irvings' attention and "poof" you were a "boiled owl".

Once a "boiled owl", one had privledges. Like telling another rider to pick up the pace, making them move over to the side of a water tank or cutting line at the porta potty. Boiled owls can offer their honest opinion about a) the judging, b) the food and c) the trail without consequence. Everyone watches them during a ride and wonders how the devil they manage it, but never questions a thing that they do. And once they "retire" from riding, they either take up judging or show up at events to see if anyone else appears to know what they are doing, which they obviously don't, so that they can offer their opinion.

"Boiled owls" have always been there, we just didn't know what to call them until Irving came along.

Down Hill and Outta Luck

One of our most adventurous trips was to take four horses to Utah to participate in the historical "Outlaw Trail" five day, two hundred and sixty five-mile endurance ride. Steve had pumped us up with stories of riding down canyons and through ghost towns. We weren't buying it. Gullible as we were, two hundred and sixty five miles was a lot of riding.

The first day of trail took us up from four thousand feet to six thousand feet. We spent the entire morning climbing. It was spectacular, but we were grateful when the trail turned downwards. We were naïve.

Both Steve and I were not using cruppers. We had never needed them, in fact, hadn't even packed them. The husband and Steve's wife did. Cruppers hold the saddle from slipping over the shoulders and neck of the horse. They are handy to have.

Half way down a particularly steep trail, I got to thinking about that crupper. My horse, Aleser, was the nicest guy, always taking each crazy situation I got him into in stride. He was being very, very careful down that trail. The footing of loose lava rock was sliding along just about as fast as we were when we made the turn out onto the ledge. The ledge offered a spectacular view of the valley below. The trail turned steeper and I felt my saddle start to move.

I had two seconds to decide to either try to stay on or try to get off. I chose the later. At the same time, Steve had the same flash of realization that a crupper was, indeed, a handy thing to have. He chose to stay on.

My landing resulted in no place to stand up. The trail was such a trough that the only place one could get purchase was in the center. Aleser was in the center. I slid not so gracefully onto my back, feet uphill, head downhill, under my kind and understanding horse. He was surprised. Hey, so was I! He had little choice but to keep moving with the other horses, so I slid down the hill under his front legs wishing all to heck that I had thought about bringing a crupper.

Steve's choice to remain on his horse proved no better. The saddle just slid right up on the horse's neck, Steve and all. The only thing keeping him from joining the valley below was the fact that his horse did not put his head down. From his vantage point, he could see me and I could see him and we could hardly help but laugh. Me under my horse, him perched on his horses ears.

The husband, riding down the trail last, and secure in his crupper, was at a loss for what to do about our predicaments. For once, he wasn't sure if he should laugh. Laughing at one's spouse in situations such as this can sometimes have serious ramifications. Realizing that we were not going to extract ourselves from our plight without help, he called out to Steve's wife, who was in the lead, to stop.

"Not hardly", she retorted, "this isn't safe to stop on!"

"Please", Steve and I whimpered, "take a look behind you."

I didn't see it, considering my position, but Dinah did a true double take when she looked over her shoulder. To her, I was completely missing and Steve appeared to be riding my horse's butt. It was a shocker. She stopped.

Grateful as I was to have finally stopped moving, I was clueless as to how to extract myself from between Alesers' legs. Steve at least had the option of rolling out of his saddle onto Alesers' rump and to the ground. The husband, two horses away could not help me. I finally reached over my head and pulled myself out by grabbing the tail of the horse in front of me. Horses are such tolerant animals.

We slid down the rest of the trail with Steve and I bracing ourselves on the tails and manes of the horses between us. I was ever so grateful to reach the bottom where I could climb safely back into the saddle. And I never forgot to bring a crupper again.

To Be or Not To Be

One could not fault the perfect summer afternoon when I set out to do some trail marking for an upcoming ride. My mount of choice was Mr. Morgan, our now retired twenty-five year old campaigner. The dogs were so happy they could sing. In fact, we were all so happy.

The Morgan hailed from a long line of horses who are in a hurry to go somewhere. "Whoa", for him, was a relative word. He would stop, give it four seconds and be back on his way. As far as he viewed it, he had "whoa'd", what more did I want? I had given up trying to explain it to him.

That said, marking trail on this horse required some skill. Stapler in one hand, arrow in the other, I would guide him to a tree, "kachunk" in the first staple and "kachunk" in the second as he swung back onto the trail. Four seconds. I had to learn to use that time wisely.

I will confess that I knew about possible evening thunderstorms before we set out. Even with the first rumblings of thunder I calculated that I could get the job done and be home before I got wet. Heck, at four seconds a tree I was moving right along. I should have sensed the hint of turning weather when the dogs, who had been gleefully sniffing and snorting through the underbrush off of the trail, rejoined me.

I was just stapling the very last arrow on the very last tree when the clap of thunder hit. I missed my second "kachunk" and almost ran down the dogs who had retreated under my horse. A rush of wind came through the woods and the sky darkened ominously. I didn't have to hear the worried panting of the dogs to know that we were in trouble.

The old horse was perhaps the most reliable mount in such a situation. I had often said that I could ride him through the gates of hell and perhaps I was about to get my chance. We were sprinting down the trail towards home, one dog in the brush to my right, the other inches ahead of me. I was calculating the seconds between thunder bursts and lightening and comparing it to the distance home. It was going to be close.

In deference to the dogs, I stopped at the brook about two miles from home. The trail would be downhill from here and pretty easy traveling. Taking their refreshment, the dogs leapt from the brook and we were off again. I must say, the Morgan was loving this, after all, we were hurrying somewhere.

At the last brook crossing I stopped again to allow the dogs another drink. Dog, not dogs. I had but one dog. Darn. By this time the wind was really whipping through the trees and while the hollow where I stood was relatively calm I could see the clearing above me. The rain came carried in a wind that dropped the temperature ten degrees in a matter of seconds. This was some storm for even the Morgan was standing still.

I was still missing a dog.

There are times when one realizes that the next few decisions one makes will dramatically affect the rest of your day. This was such a time. I could go back up the trail in search of the dog or continue home in hope that she was tucked in safely and would return home when the storm passed. No one knew I was out in the storm, the husband being away and the neighbors figuring I was too smart to be in a dumb place like this. I agonized over my options.

I went home.

At the bottom of my driveway I was greeted by two large trees lying across the way. Further up I saw the top of a pine tree splayed across the fence and found the barn without power. It was only then that I appreciated being in that hollow when the wind hit.

But what about the dog.

This wasn't just any dog. It was the husbands dog. Not that she was any more valuable for that, but that the husband claimed but one animal for his own and she was it. The horses, the cats, the goat and goose and the ferret were ours. But this dog was his. And for good reason.

As a boy, the husband grew up as the youngest on a very busy farm. There were animals all about but they were working animals, not pets. It wasn't until we were married that I brought animals into the house. The husband embraced this concept somewhat tentively until a wonderful Australian Shepard puppy, Blueberry took him on. That was it, they were a pair for life.

It had been only a little over a year ago when Blueberry left us. Despondant that he would never again have such a wonderful companion, the husband had been a bit tough to live with. One fine winter day, a neighbor arrived with a squirrely tri-colored little mutt jammed between her two golden retrievers in the rear seat of her truck. Seems she had a moment of weakness while vacationing in Antigia and decided to rescue an island dog. No matter that it was February in Vermont and that the transition had to be somewhat of a shock for the poor dog.

Used to complete freedom on the island, this staying in the house stuff was driving the dog crazy. And my friend. We were the solution. Just take her for the weekend and see if you like her, she said. Well, that was a suckers bet, we were not the kind of people who could "try" an animal. We were practicing addicts as demonstrated by the cornicopea of creatures that lived with us. Some friend.

And so Meant To Be came to live with us and willfully, gleefully, amazingly filled the space that Blueberry left behind. The husband returned to his pleasant self and could often be overheard talking to his dog with full belief that she hung on every word.

It was impossible for me to visualize the husband should I have to tell him that I lost his dog in the woods. It would certainly be grounds for divorce.

Slogging back to the house, I changed my clothes and sat by the window in the waning light yearning for the sight of a jaunty little dog trotting up the driveway. I was feeling completely helpless. As I squeezed back the tears, a ray of light came through the sky and the rain, as suddenly as it started, just stopped. What had seemed like encroaching night, suddenly lit up to reveal dusk with perhaps another hour of light.

For the second time that afternoon I found myself at that decision making point which would either make or break my day. I could grab a horse, ride back into the woods and even if trees were down, bushwhack back to the last place I saw her. About two miles out. But if she was hurt, I would have no way to bring her home. If I took the four-wheeler I had no recourse but to walk the two miles if I encountered down trees. I had thirty seconds to work through each scenario; I took the four-wheeler. It had lights.

To say that the trip back up that trail was an adventure would not be giving the experience full credit. With the wind gone I was able to yell at the top of my lungs for the dog. "To Be", To Be". Nothing. Surely she knew the sound of the four-wheeler and would come running. Nothing. It started to rain again. And the hour of light gave out. Darn.

I was practically feeling my way along the trail to the location at the brook where I had last seen her. I shut down the motor and called again. Nothing. It occurred to me that, again, I was out in the woods and no one knew. Then it occurred to me that bear have been sighted in the area, and while I was not particulary concerned about being attacked by a bear, it did tickle my imagination.

Just then the saplings behind me cracked with the noise of something moving fast. As I turned to the right, a black form sailed over my head, sliding into a crash landing next to me. Then it kissed me in the face. To Be!

We had a long talk on the way home about not staying with the group and how much she had worried me. Accustomed to the husband, she hung on every word but didn't hear a thing. Delighted to be back home, she resumed life as if nothing happened. When the husband called to ask about my day, I mentioned nothing. I would wait for another time to tell him the story. Then I had a stiff drink and went to bed.

Frosty Fifty

The weather report was forewarning us of plummeting temperatures, heavy rain and possible snow in high altitudes. I left for a fifty-mile endurance ride outside of Harrisburg, Pennsylvania anyway.

I arrived to seasonal fall temperatures and settled into setting up camp for my horse and myself. This was early in my endurance riding career, so camp consisted of portable electric fence for my horse and a sleeping bag in the dressing room of my trailer for me. I had splurged for an awning on the trailer that would provide shelter for the horse should it rain. It was actually pretty cozy.

The rain started that afternoon. So the weatherman was right. It was still warm and we all adjusted our outerwear accordingly. By dinner, we could barely hear ourselves talk for the din on the roof from the driving rain. I wasn't so amused about that weatherman anymore. Suddenly, the noise stopped.

"Hey", it's stopped raining," someone yelled as they went for the door.

We stood silent as we peered out into the twilight of drifting snowflakes. I really, really, was upset about that weatherman now.

Endurance riders are a tough lot. Nothing bothers them. Not heat, not rain, not mud, not a little snowstorm. But I heard a few whimpers.....

I had already agreed to watch a friend's horse overnight as they were staying in a motel. Some deal. They probably didn't even know it was snowing as they watched cable TV and ate take-out pizza.

As I adjusted the blankets on the horses, the snow really started to come down. It floated on top of the sea of water and mud caused by the earlier deluge, making it look like whipped cream on hot chocolate. My horse was from Georgia. Up until this point, he didn't know what snow was, but he was learning fast.

The weight of the wet snow on my electric fence had it sagging almost to the ground. I did my best to prop it up, but the mud had its way. Once I had the horses secure, I turned to enter my trailer but to my dismay, a sagging awning blocked the door. So much wet snow had accumulated on it that I feared it would collapse. I grabbed a broom and within an hour had it cleared off.

Finally in the sanctity of my dressing room, I turned my propane heater on "high" and stripped off my cold wet clothes. Clothes. Calculating that I would get the rest of them wet riding the next day, I had only one dry set left to go home in. That was the moment I started to wonder just what the heck I was doing here instead of in a nice cozy motel, or better yet, in the comfort of home.

I decided to take one more peek outside before settling into my pleasant warm sleeping bag. The first push of the door indicated that the awning was once again sagging against the weight of the wet snow. I closed my eyes, picturing the collapsed awning trapping me in my dressing room with no one the wiser. Reluctantly, I realized that I was going to have to get up all night to clear the snow in order for that not to happen. I began to whimper.

In order to preserve my diminishing supply of dry clothing, I performed my snow clearing task in nothing but a raincoat and pair of carrot bags on my feet. The carrot bags were emptied of their contents and secured on my feet with rubber bands before I jammed my feet into already soaking sneakers. I thought that rather clever.

My pilgrimage outside every few hours revealed a surreal landscape of flocked snow on trees, fences and once green grass. An occasional snort from a horse told what they thought of the situation. As the temperature dropped, my sleeping bag, despite boasting that it was good for temperatures down to minus ten below, lost it's coziness. I pilfered my tack box until I was layered beneath a mountain of horse coolers, some of which retained that earthy odor of sweat and horse that is not so bad unless you are trying to sleep.

My fellow endurance riders were not doing much better. One had decided to put her horse inside the trailer, resulting in a night's worth of pawing and banging making her sleep, and those near her, impossible. Another decided to get out before it got any worse. His attempts to pull through the mud dug him so deep that he could not open his truck door. And the poor trail manager. She had marked the trail with, of all things, white chalk! The only ones that slept peacefully through the night were my friends in their warm, dry motel room.

By dawn, the snow had frozen stiff to everything it touched. My fence was weighted to the ground, but my horse was so bewildered that he dare not move an inch He looked like the statue of "The End of the Trail", sans the Indian.

I didn't even bother getting up when my alarm went off. My friends, fresh from their comfy night in the motel, swung open my trailer door to find me still in the sack.

"Get up!" they chirped.

Not so amused with their bright enthusiasm, I retorted, "Easy for you to say coming from a "real" nights sleep. I am cold, I am tired and I am ugly!"

They left.

It was the first, and last, time I whimped out at a ride. And, it was the first, and the last time, I ignored a weather report.

Mr. Magoo

I did not want a ferret. The ferret did not want me. Little did either of that have to do with how we met. I had just lost my ferret, Dulcinea, and was just not ready for another squeaky weasel. The ferret was caught up in a divorce and a move where pets were not allowed. It was actually the husband who said yes. The man never ceases to amaze me.

The ferret arrived in a car stuffed to the roof with ferret possessions. A cage, a long tube for slithering, two litter boxes, three bags of food, two tins of treats, a summer blanket, a winter blanket, a stuffed octopus, a second long tube for slithering, a box of specially designed ferret-safe Styrofoam peanuts for snorkeling, and a big bag of toys. I was almost embarrassed to show them where my ferret had lived.

Ushered into the house, the ferret watched as his people set up his new home just the way he would like it. He watched the door every time they left and I could see his relief every time they returned. This was going to be hard.

I didn't expect this ferret to be all too excited about having a new home. I figured his lethargic attitude had to do with the loss of his family and the newness of me. I would pluck him from his cage and he would limply lie on my arm as I pet and scratched him. No reaction. He remained limp on my arm as I carried him about. Not normal. I would put him down on the floor, he would shake himself off, trundle to his cage and go back to sleep. It was darn right depressing to watch.

Five months later there was little progress. "How's the ferret?" would ask the husband. "Asleep". Fact was that I would wake him up in the morning; he would climb into the clothes hamper and sleep all day. I would wake him up in the evening and he would trundle to his cage and sleep all night. I even had a sign on the clothes washer "Check for Ferret Before Washing". For all I knew, he could be capable of sleeping through an entire wash cycle.

Any ferret prowess was lost with this guy. Having had his nails trimmed regularly as a baby, he never did learn to climb. And it didn't look like was going to learn. Placed on the bed, he would look over the edge to the floor in confused panic. First he would try to get down forwards, then backwards, then forwards until he lost his balance and flopped with a thump on the floor. "What was that?" would query the husband. "Just the ferret". "Oh, glad he is so playful." Well, not quite.

Every time I picked this guy up, tickled his belly and waited for something other than a yawn, I was so disappointed. Where was the "joi de vie" of the ferrets I had previously known. Was he so despondent about loosing his family or was this ferret a dud.

Then we got the kitten.

Gypsy Rose Lee lived up to her namesake in more ways than one. Her presence filled the house. Completely convinced that she was the cutest thing on earth she bounced and flounced through the hierarchy of the house without a hitch. The husband no exception.

She and her littermate, Sister Mary Agnes (black with a white bib, of course) were the result of another trip to our conniving friend in Pennsylvania who always seemed to have kittens available. The husband arrived home with the two, proudly declaring that the lice had already been taken care of so all we had to do was deworm them. They did their detox in the barn and were adjusting well when Gypsy appeared in the house.

"I want my own cat," declared the husband. I looked at the three lovely housecats already in place. "Not them," he said, "they like only you." "Cats just like me," I returned. "Well, I want at least one to like me", he said in a somewhat defensive manner. Fine with me. That lasted less than a week. The husband even took to sleeping with the kitten in the guest room with the door closed but Gypsy clung to me all day. "You're a dog person", I tried to explain when he realized he was defeated. Still, he pouted.

Somewhat unfair to the husband in Gypsy's attraction to me was that I smelled of ferret. Fascinating! The ferret, still devoid of a name since he had to have a personality before he could get a name, was not thinking he would have to change his routine just because of a kitten. So wrong.

Gypsy would stare a hole through the laundry hamper every time the ferret moved. Eventually, he would climb out to find a most excitable feline blocking his way to the comforts of his cage where a little supper and a drink would precede further napping. He either had to run, which his fat little body didn't do very well, or stand his ground until the kitten got bored, which was not happening fast enough. Lots of chatter, lots of circles, lots of rolling and flopping on each other. Darned right exhausting.

The Mr. Magoo name came from what one would have thought impossible for a ferret to do, to squint. From where ever he was hiding, the head would pop out and a quick survey of the area made in order to determine if Gypsy might be lurking in the area. Then a mad dash, often not successful, to the next possible hiding place onroute to wherever the ferret was going. It was best not to be in that path when the two collided.

 It was during one such episode when the two escaped the bedroom, continuing their romp through the house. Fate would have it that the cellar door was open and true to form, Mr. Magoo missed the first step and rolled ploppity-plop into the cellar. We didn't see him for three days.

Even the husband was becoming distraught over the missing weasel. "He's probably asleep somewhere," I said rather sarcastically. After all, sleeping was Mr. Magoo's best talent. The husband took it upon himself to mention this to a fellow Morgan owner and ferret fan. "Oh, " she laughed, "our ferret was AWOL for almost a week once. We finally spotted him in the basement and followed him to a cozy little hole he made for himself. He still goes there from time to time." "He's loose in the house?" said the husband. "Sure, we gave up trying to keep him contained and it totally solved our mouse and squirrel problems."

"What a novel idea, a free-range ferret", I commented after hearing the story from the husband. Where was he when I had told him about my first ferret, Mabel, the one who lived in the second drawer on the right in my desk? No matter, I hadn't presented the idea and I could see that the husband was thinking this a solution to the scratchy noises in the walls that he knew to be either mice or squirrels. Mr. Magoo was on his own.

Having slept off his adventure in the basement, Mr. Magoo's face would appear peeking out from a low piece of furniture in an effort to negotiate the safest path back through the house to his cage, and food, without encountering Gypsy. She was always waiting for him.

The moment of truth had arrived. Either Magoo was going to be hounded forever or he was going to have to wake up, join life and get down to fighting shape. Which he did.

The two worked out an "arrangement" that eventually bloomed into a strong bond of friendship. Often as not, they would share at the water dish or roll playfully across the rug. They found each other entertaining, and the true Mr. Magoo emerged.

Unlike my previous ferrets, Magoo remained very laid back about life. The vacuum cleaner did not send him into frenzy and he loved taking a shower and shampoo (although he failed to master how to jump into the tub). He never did learn how to climb, or perhaps it was simply too much work. But he finally mastered the stairs, which was a relief, for I wondered just how much tumpity-tumps a ferret could take.

Mr. Magoo had two passions. One was my iRobot Scooba floor-washing robot. Nothing could fascinate a ferret more than a humming, spinning, water producing machine. He could chase it or ride it or roll on the newly washed floor. The little tune it played, tat-dada, as it started up brought him scurrying whenever I ran it, which was a lot during mud season. He would scratch at it as if to unearth whoever was inside running the thing. It was like watching a ferret run a Zamboni during intermission at a hockey game!

The second passion was bubble wrap. It mattered little what was contained in the bubble wrap as once a rather pricey piece of Royal Dolton china was dragged through the house and in the process of being stuffed under the stove just as the husband rescued it. I thought it quite industrious of my former couch potato ferret but the husband thought otherwise.

If bubble wrap was not available, pieces of paper from the office trash basket would do. Not being a ferret, it was hard for me to appreciate the differences in pieces of paper, as did Mr. Magoo. He would climb into the basket and sort with intensity for the right piece. Each would be pawed at, sniffed, picked up in the mouth and either discarded or whisked away down the hall to under the stove.

Understandably, the husband had a valid concern about papers being stored underneath a gas stove. I was pretty sure someone at the gas-stove factory had recognized the possibility of a ferret nesting under it and had installed the proper precautions. But I agreed to fish under the stove with a yardstick before lighting the oven. It never hurts to be careful.

Mr. Magoo did not think much of this procedure. He had copped quite an attitude since his days in the laundry hamper and it was not uncommon for him to grip a piece of paper firmly in his teeth as one of us attempted to pull it out. Sometimes dinner was late.

While the yardstick did a good job removing the papers, it was useless on a ferret. Just to show us that those factory guys did know what they were doing, he remained under the stove once when it was lit. We freaked out. A quick peek with the flashlight showed him curled up directly under the oven part. If anyone wants underwriting for gas stoves, Mr. Magoo is available.

As it turned out, the husband became a ferret fan. I would have to hide my smirk as I listened to him tell friends of Magoo's latest adventures. One morning I actually found the husband and the ferret in bed together. Of course that didn't last too long because Mr. Magoo fell off of the bed. Some things never change.

Shopping for a Star

One of the sure signs of a horse addict is that when asked how many horses they have, they have trouble answering. Horse addicts don't see their horses in numbers because that would be an admission to their addiction. Add to this the complicated way in which horse addicts attempt to count horses. If the horse is pregnant, do you count one or two? If you own a horse, but have it retired at someone else's barn, do you count that one? What about the horse you have on lease? Or the one you are thinking about buying? Or selling? And at just what point are too many horses anyway? See?

The horse addict is faced with the constant fear that someday they might find themselves without a horse to ride. That does not mean that the barn is empty, but the horse might be too young, too old, too pregnant or too lame to ride, a condition that could happen to any horse at any time. So, to cover the odds, more than one horse is necessary and it follows that the more horses one has, the odds are in the horse addicts favor.

But there is a point where too many horses produces guilt. Guilt because the horse addict is not doing anything "productive" with that horse simply because there are not enough hours in the day. Obviously it is a good animal, otherwise it would not be in the horse addicts possession. Horse addicts spend a lifetime honing their skills in procuring only quality horses. Horse addicts hate to see a good animal going to waste!

Now enters the dilemma of justifying keeping "X" number of horses in the horse addicts stable. Every horse addict has some kind of passion, whether it be fox hunting or endurance riding or horse shows or breeding. Every horse in the horse addicts barn has exhibited some signs of talent for such. The horse addict always has a "star" horse, the one that is better than all of the rest and brings great pleasure to the horse addict. But the horse addict also knows that this will not last forever, so they are forever keeping their eye out for potential "stars" to add to the barn. If the horse addict has been at this for a while, there are past "stars" in the barn that deserve retirement, offspring of past "stars" that will take forever to grow up to become a "star" and those that failed to be "stars" but are so nice otherwise that they have to stay.

Even with a barn full of "stars", the fact remains that the horse addict is still fearful that someday they might find themselves without a horse to ride. So they never turn down an opportunity to horse shop.

I don't feel too badly about my horse addiction as I have a friend who has twenty seven horses and is forever shopping for a new horse because she keeps breeding them and has nothing to ride.

But I suffer from "the fear" and therefore keep my eye out for possible "stars" to fill my barn with. It is one thing to casually look at horses when you already have your barn full of "stars". You can be picky and talk yourself out of just about anything by rationalizing that you don't have the time, space, need or money for another horse. But even with a barn full of "stars, one day you wake up to the realization that suddenly one horse is getting old, another not talented enough and another needs time off...and the heart gripping fear of not having a horse to ride, even if one is projecting a year off, grabs control.

Whenever I feel that I NEED a horse, I can't find one. I look and look and travel all over and read ads, call people, view videos and nothing fits the bill. Drowning in my feeling of panic, I usually hit bottom before finding the right one.

Hitting bottom is a lot like thinking that no one is going to ask you to the prom. Then, after hearing from your mother and friends that the prom is nothing but a pumped up dance and who cares if you go or not, the phone rings.

So, of course, my next new horse started with a phone call.

"Hi, I understand you are looking for a horse?" chirps a fellow horse addict.

The husband rolls his eyes, he figures that by now people in third world countries know I am looking for a horse!

"Well, I know of a horse that has been for sale for a while and just learned that he flunked the vet, but don't take that too seriously because the good thing is that the price has dropped and you could pick him up very reasonably."

Since I have now hit bottom, I don't say "thanks ...but", I continue the conversation hoping that the husband hasn't heard any of this.

"He's a local horse (go figure, I've been all over the country looking!) so you could work with him a bit before deciding. I looked at him last year and really liked him, (so why didn't you buy him?) but (here it comes!) I don't think I have the talent that you have to bring out his potential." (he must be a real nut case!).

Getting directions, I hang up and meet the husband with that "oh no" look so I soften it up a bit in order to get him to go see the horse with me. He knows I have "rules" about buying horses and I know that I am about to break a few.

We ended up taking along two other horse addict friends to see the horse as it seems the phone call to me also was made to them. If I didn't want him, they were in position to pounce. They already had twenty some horses so I thought it a bit unfair as I was the one who had hit bottom. But I also knew the rules of horse shopping and none had been broken.

The horse in question was stabled at a breeding farm. There were mares and babies and stallions everywhere. He had been purchased as a package deal with his sister who was as cute and pretty as any mare could be. He was tall, leggy, gaunt and clueless. He was scared to death of the stallion, who wanted to kill him simply on the grounds that he was not a mare. Moving the horse to the barn at a run to avoid the charging stallion made for considerable entertainment on our part. I could see why the owner was desperate to remove this horse from her care!

What I saw in the barn was a big five year old baby with incredible legs and feet and the potential to fill out into a very handsome horse. Hmmm. He stood quietly to be saddled and seemed all business as he was walked out to the riding area. So, I kept thinking…where's the problem? Why have so many people passed on this horse?

I tactfully asked about the failure of this horse to pass the vet check. It seems that it was an issue of the horse failing to submit to the vet check. Ah, I said, starting to see the problem.

The rider shimmied up onto his back like a monkey and rode him around for several minutes with no issues. Hmmm. Yes, I said, I would like to ride him. I caught the eye of the husband and agreed that he should head the horse while I mounted. The horse was so tall I needed a mounting block. The mounting block was obviously the first mounting block the horse had ever encountered which produced a similar reaction from him as did a charging stallion. The problem was becoming clearer by the minute.

The owner was very apologetic and explained that the horse had only been lightly ridden and was really not to be considered "broke". No kidding. After two aborted attempts to mount, the husband implored me not to try again. But, I was a horse addict that had hit bottom and was seeing potential "stardom" in this horse. I WANTED this horse to work and I was going to break one of my rules unless I mounted him right then and there. I had never purchased a horse I hadn't sat upon and I was not about to do that now.

So, up I went the third time and to my surprise landed on a very quiet back. No quivering, no jumpiness, no fear, just pure ignorance of what I was doing there. I managed to walk him around in several circles then figured I should not push it and hopped off. Whew.

I bought him.

Then I went home and suffered a night of buyers regret which every horse addict has right after purchasing a new animal. The only one excited was the husband, which was weird, because he usually doesn't get wound up in my purchases,. But he too saw the potential for "stardom" in this horse, only he wasn't the one that had to bring it out!

I should have videoed the circus that surrounded the attempts to load the horse on my trailer. Yes, the owner stated, he has been trailered many times (because he had already had many owners in his short years of life!) I still had the check in my hand, so it was THEIR horse they were loading, not mine. As the battle to load the horse ensued, I got to see a more of "the problems" that were going to have to be dealt with and was getting a big lump in my stomach. It was not too late to back out...he was not on the trailer yet!

As I watched the circus, I had a big fight with myself. You know, the kind of fight your conscious self has with your idealistic self. It went like this...

"What are you thinking buying this horse!"

"I am thinking he has "star" potential."

"Well, babe, you must want it bad because this horse has no manners and could hurt someone...like you! He's an idiot!"

"Well...yeah, but I have bought other idiots and they turned out OK."

"Name one!"

"Aleser!"

"He was not an idiot."

"He was unrideable!"

"That does not count, he had been abused by a trainer and simply needed to get over it. The difference was that he didn't rear straight up and paw the air like this one!"

"Yeah, that's not so good, but he's just a spoiled baby and I can fix it.

"Right, one of these days you aren't going to "fix" a horse and that will leave you in a real dilemma and you know it."

"I know, I know you are right...but I'm buying him anyway." My stomach hurt.

With that the horse leapt into my trailer and had the tail gate slammed shut behind him by a very relieved owner. I handed the check to his now former owner and four of her grateful relatives let out a big sigh. He was my problem now.

I gave the Tyger several weeks to adjust to his new home. He didn't seem to think he needed much adjusting, probably because he had had so many different homes before this, he didn't care. But I wanted him to be comfortable and I wanted time to study him.

Seems he was a brat. From the get go he pushed the other horses around even though he was the new guy. He would swing his butt and back into any horse that dared challenge him. He was suspicious of the barn even at feeding time and bolted out into the middle of the pasture at any strange noise. He didn't give a hoot about me, in fact, I was something to be avoided.

The only way I could catch him was to maneuver him into a paddock alone and then put feed in the stall. He ate like it was his last meal, gulping down the grain as he ran to the stall gate, testing it's strength to hold him in. I then had to bribe my way to his head with carrots or mints before I could loop a rope over his neck.

Amazingly, once I had him caught, he accepted me with no problem. I could brush him, pick his feet, place a saddle on him, cross tie him with no issues. I just could not move him. As if I kept a raging stallion in every corner, he moved ready to run at the slightest provocation. He cringed when I hosed him down, he spooked when I filled a bucket from the water hydrant, and about fell down if the goose flapped her wings. Just where had this boy been for his five years?

Visions of "stardom" dimmed considerably when I started Tygers training. He simply did not get it! Every day I would head for the barn with a seemingly simple task in mind for him to master knowing full well that he would find a way to make a mess of it. After three months, he was no where near the point of being ridden. Even attempts to rub his face and fuss with him were met with disinterest. I was discouraged, only the husband held out hope.

"The good ones are always tough", he said, "stick with it"

I think he read that in some book, because I had had a lifetime of good ones that were very easy to train. What the heck did he know!

All I could hear was my conscience snickering "I told you so!"

I needed help. He needed help. I knew of a trainer who oversaw a "horse boot camp" type of establishment that would either make or break this horse. I had never sent a horse to a trainer that I could not handle myself, but this was an exception. The trainer understood my position and was willing to take a try with him.

First, I had to get him there. Oh, boy, that meant the trailer. I told the trainer not to expect us for a while.

Trailer training required the assistance of the husband and we both knew what we were in for. Tyger had fought with his handlers every time he had been loaded so he was ready for us. Our job was to change the game and not fight back. His first antics at seeing the trailer were ignored, which confused him but didn't change his attitude. It took all afternoon, but he finally went quietly into the trailer. Normally, the next training session would show improvement, but not with this horse. Every day we went through the same routine and every day it took hours to load him. Even the husband was beginning to agree that this horse was something "special".

Every horse trainer will admit that there are those that don't get it. Kinda like teaching a kid to read, if the first method fails, try another and another until they figure it out. I had been through all the tricks of the trade, Tyger didn't "join up", he didn't even "listen up" and I was about to "give up".

I agonized as to what to do with this big dumb horse. He wasn't trained or wanting to be trained. Plus he looked awful. Even after four months of good grass, plenty of feed and proper care his coat was still dull and his body gaunt. We had come to rather dislike each other, given the constant battle we were in. He had one last chance.

So, the day before I left for Europe I devoted the afternoon to loading him into the trailer and delivered "Mr. Special" to the trainer. I figured that my being gone would keep me from sneaking over to the trainers to see how things were going. Being a horse person, I secretly hated the idea that someone else could get from this horse what I had failed to do. I left the trainer with the understanding that if Tyger didn't work it out, to sell him. I left hearing hooves banging on the stall amid screams from within. Perhaps he missed me? More likely he was mad at having to do yet something else that he really didn't want to do. I left not knowing if I would ever see him again.

The poor trainer almost shot him after three days of continuous banging, screaming and poor behavior. The trainer was thinking I was the smart one, dropping the horse off then leaving the country like that. Then the darndest thing happened. He stopped. And he allowed himself to be caught. And lunged. And saddled. And by the end of those three weeks he was cantering around the ring with a rider on his back. The trainer would have liked to take the credit, but was honest in saying that the horse simply experienced a revelation all on his own.

Perhaps he knew he had only one more chance?

The big shiny chestnut horse, the one with the lofty gait that catches everyone's eye, the one with a pile of champion ribbons to his credit, is the same horse that I bought on a gut feeling that day years ago. He hops into trailers and travels like a pro. He is a real pet and easy to ride and train and has the most incredible gaits. He outshines every horse he comes up against, not just with his good looks, but with his confidence, for this horse now knows he's a "star".

We're Only Human

We were on a scavenger hunt on Mackinaw Island, Michigan. It was part of the American Driving Society's annual meeting's activities. Mackinaw is unique in that it allows no cars, transportation being provided by horse and buggy. It was a perfect place for our meet.

We had rented a "U-Aim-'Em" at the local livery for the scavenger hunt. There were six of us, a surrey with a fringe on top and Red. Red was the horse. Other than the husband and I, there was a four-in-hand driver from California, a tandem and a pair driver from Michigan and the executive director of the Carriage Association of America. We thought, between us, that we knew what we were doing.

Being competitive types, we were trying to be competitive in the scavenger hunt. We studied the map, divided up tasks, planned our route and were off. Well, we were off at a walk. Red walked. Red did not trot, nor did Red go anywhere that he was not supposed to go. We, being a surrey load of educated and able drivers, commenced to try to change Red's mind.

We tried the word "trot".

Nothing.

Perhaps he speaks French?, suggested one. "Or German?"

Red was a big draft type horse, more likely he knew farm terms.

"Cluck", we went, "cluck, cluck, cluck."

Nothing.

"Perhaps we should tap him with the whip?", volunteered another.

Nothing.

"Tap some more", was voiced.

More tapping produced the raised rear end of Red. He was not amused and we got the point. We were annoying, but not stupid.

"I'll get out and try to lead him," offered the more determined of the group.

There was the amusing sight of a person running alongside a big red horse that had no intention of acknowledging his presence. This effort produced a lot of cat calls and laughs, but no trot.

We had run out of ideas.

Red was in control.

What Red knew that we did not know was his job. Red worked the streets of Mackinaw Island all summer, taking people that hadn't the faintest clue how to drive a horse safely around. The people were happy, Red's owner was happy and Red was happy.

Then come along a carriage load of idiots who wanted to change everything just because they thought that they knew something. Why should Red trust us? Why should he throw all of his training away just because we said so? Who the heck were we to him?

So Red pulled us, at a walk, everywhere he knew to go, which was NOT where the scavenger hunt went, despite our entreaties. We gave up trying and amused ourselves by singing "Surrey with the Fringe on Top" although we didn't know all of the words.

Red was typical of many horses. He had been trained to do a specific job and that was what he did. If you wanted to train a horse to do something new, you had to first get their attention, and respect. People can be the same way.

What sets certain horses apart from others is when they come to figure things out, even before you do. Horses can overcome their natural fears, their natural reactive instincts because their connection to man is even greater. Sometimes this can be taught, but sometimes it's just there.

In Red's case, he had been taught how to behave. But in Kharis' case, it was just there.

Kharis was the product of a carefully selected breeding program for black Arabians. He came out bright chestnut, almost orange, with a big white blaze. He looked like Mr. Ed. Oops, not black. I have always held to "what is one mans garbage is another man's treasure." They tossed him out of the barn and we happily scooped him up.

Being an Arabian, he was considered "hot blooded". But a more a gentle soul could not be found. This horse, who never won any championships or had his picture in any magazines, touched more lives in a positive way than any other horse I knew. He was a born teacher. Tolerant, patient, kind, rewarding.

There was absolutely no reason why Kharis did not bolt when the carriage hit him from behind while going down our barn driveway. Instinct should have mandated it. He had in his care my young niece, who lovingly rode him every day, but didn't know much about hooking up a carriage. She had not adjusted the breeching correctly, so when the carriage came down the hill, it moved further and further towards the horse until it banged with each step into his hind legs.

Any other horse would have bolted, kicked or run. But Kharis continued down the hill with the carriage banging his legs until he reached the barn safely. He understood someone had made a mistake. He understood he was to take care of my niece.

Sometimes horses give us a break for being human. I want to stand up right now to say how thankful I am for that.

Munching Under My Window

The soft sounds of a horse chewing grass floated through my window and into my sleep. Half awake, I knew the sound to be coming from my retired horse, Kharis, who was enjoying a midnight snack at my window.

Vermont offers the senses very short, but intense, pleasures. Snow shoeing under a full moon through wooded paths with shadows thrown before you. Swimming in a pond at sunset on an August eve with crayfish nibbling at one's toes. The Northern Lights dancing across the sky in blazing neon fashion in the middle of the night. Dew ridden nights with Kharis sleeping peacefully under my window. I cannot choose which to be my greatest pleasure.

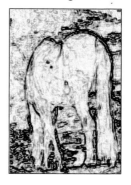

Night in Vermont offers up it's own special beauty. Stars take over the sky to a mezmorizing extent. Drawn by the night sky, we would often dine at dusk on our stone patio and watch day turn to night as the nights softness changes our world. In spring, the rrrurpp of the tree frogs was almost deafening, to be replaced by the peep of the spring peepers and eventually by the deep errpp of the bull frog. Humming birds swooped past us as we finished our dinner to be replaced by bats when it became dark.

On more than one occasion I would lie back in the grass, the dampness cooling my back, and listen to the sounds of the Vermont night. Added to the chorus was the sound of Kharis, roaming free on our farm, munching grass and snorting his opinion from time to time. Under the moonlight he was like a mystical creature, one borne on wings, not one of this world. He would come to me and nuzzle my hand, offering me affection as if he could give me any wish I wanted. All I could wish for was that he never left me, that he kept my treasured summer nights with his presence. For had he shown himself to me with a unicorn horn I would not have been surprised, for he was to me magic.

Jane's Last Ride

There are all kinds of ways to pay tribute to a fellow horseperson when they leave us. Most never want a big funeral, rather a gathering of friends, perhaps in a pasture full of horses, where our spirits are most comfortable.

I wrote this for my dear friend, Jane. She was a matter of fact type of woman who lived her life to it's fullest. She loved her horses, something that was at times a difficult thing for her family to understand. It's hard when you are a kid or a husband and feel that you are competing with a horse for someone's attention. But in the end, it was the realization that it was because of the horse that this person was who she was. And that is what I wrote for her family, and for her.

Because of the horse she had compassion. She knew that those without voices to speak needed to be cared for. At times she spoke for them.

Because of the horse she learned responsibility. Regardless of the weather you must still care for those you have the stewardship of. There were no "days off" just because you don't feel like it. Jane didn't listen to excuses.

Because of horses she understood competition. She compelled us to win with humility and lose with dignity.

Because of horses she learned sportsmanship and saw to it that everyone around her held to her high level. To Jane, everyone who competed fairly was a winner.

Because of horses she saw the beauty of this world. On their backs she was carried to moments of splendor and she encouraged us all to get out there and do the same.

Because of horses she understood risk. She placed her foot in the stirrup knowing that what she would gain in the experience far outweighed anything that could happen. When we fell off, she was the first to tell us to get back on.

Because of horses she knew that choices made today can effect what happens years down the road. She reminded us of that each time we made a mistake.

Because of the horse she understood the value of money. Every dollar was translated into bales of hay, bags of feed and weighed against putting gas in the truck. Jane could make the buffalos on a nickel squeak.

Because of the horse she was not afraid of getting dirty. Appearances don't matter to most of the breathing things in the world we live in. She knew that horses do not care if you try to impress them.

Jane never wasted a minute to share what she learned in life. She took the power of the horse and made sure we learned from it too.